Say the Le You're Smiling

by
Paul Duffin

Cover design by Claire Duffin

©2018 Paul Duffin

Other books by Paul Duffin

NOT TOO BAD

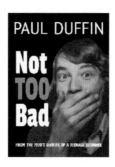

From the 1970's diaries of a teenage Brummie
All proceeds to Guide Dogs

"enjoy this sparkling piece of modern day local history made fun" – JH

AND THE CRICKET WAS GOOD TOO!

Enjoy the fun and laughter following the England cricket team around the world on nine of their tours.
All proceeds to Sense, the Deafblind charity

"an enjoyable read full of laughs"
The Cricketer Magazine May 2018

Both books available on Amazon in Kindle and paperback

PREFACE

Since becoming severely sight and hearing impaired, I turned to writing in aid of charity. My first book "Not Too Bad" (based on the diaries on a teenage Brummie) was launched on Amazon in November 2016 and has so far sold over 250 copies and raised over £1600 for Guide Dogs UK. My second book "And The Cricket Was Good Too!" (based on my nine tours following the England cricket team around the world) was launched in November 2017 and has so far sold nearly 200 copies and raised over £1300 for SENSE, the deafblind charity.

This book is hopefully an amusing account of my career with the Leeds Permanent Building Society from joining at the end of 1974 to the merger with the Halifax in August 1995. The charity this time is Prostate Cancer UK.

I have had lots of help with this book particularly my two trusted editors Liz Lavender and Andy Bates. My wife Sue and friend Dennis Skinner have also been a great help as has my daughter Claire who has designed the cover. I have received many stories from old Leeds colleagues and hope I have been able to include them either in the main body or in the "other Leeds stories" section. My sincere apologies if I have left anyone out. Also, a big thank you to all those who donated in advance raising nearly £200 for Prostate Cancer UK.

I have tried to be careful not to embarrass or offend anyone and where I felt a little unsure have left out names or changed them.

Paul Duffin
November 2018

INTRODUCTION

On leaving Central Grammar School in the summer of 1971 with 6 O' levels I joined Wragge & Co, the large Birmingham solicitors' practice, as a trainee legal executive (LExec).

I spent a very useful three years learning the art of conveyancing and passing the LExec exams to Associate level. Even more important was learning how to mix with people of all ages and backgrounds. I think of those times as my alternative university years.

By the summer of 1974 I found myself at a crossroads. The three other trainees I started with had all made the bold decision to leave and set foot on the challenging road to becoming fully qualified lawyers. Until 2011 fully qualified LExecs (Fellows) could not become partners, which we all saw as a real career block.

I had a choice to make; stay and qualify as a Fellow, leave and try to qualify as a lawyer or leave for a new career. I decided on the last option as I saw the time and effort it took to be a qualified lawyer and was not happy to stay at my current level. I looked at several avenues and came close to accepting a very tempting offer from the Wellcome Foundation but backed out at the last minute, as I would have to relocate to who knows where.

The Leeds' advertisement for a management trainee in the Birmingham Evening Mail immediately struck a chord as there appeared to be no barriers to promotion. I was also used to being on the other side of mortgages and it was local.

Two interviews were held at the branch on Temple Row both conducted by the Manager, Norman Weatherhead. All went well with the only surprise being the possibility of working at Acocks Green branch.

Everything about the job felt right with plenty of opportunities in a rapidly expanding business. I accepted their offer and was looking forward to becoming Chief
Clerk at Acocks Green.

CHAPTER 1
ACOCKS GREEN BRANCH
NOV 1974 TO MAY 1976

ACOCKS GREEN

The Birmingham suburb ACOCKS GREEN (referred to locally as "The Green") lies just over 5 miles to the south of the city centre. It is named after the Acocks family who built a large house in the area in 1370. It is now part of the Yardley constituency which, until fairly recently, was a swing seat (won by whoever was in power). It is a blue-collar area with the highest percentage of people working in manufacturing.

The only famous person from The Green is the comedian Jasper Carrott. He was born in Shaftmoor Lane in 1945 and educated at Moseley Grammar School.

FEELING AT HOME

On leaving the solicitors Wragge & Co I decided to take a week off before starting at the Leeds on Monday 2nd December 1974. My new manager, Trevor Jones, rang and invited me to pop in during that week to "break the ice".

Before I made my debut I did some research on my new employers. Of the hundreds of building societies around at the time the Leeds was wrestling for fourth place with the Woolwich. The top three were the Halifax, which was the largest, ahead of Abbey National in second place, and with the Nationwide coming in third.

Despite the UK economy being in trouble following a miners' strike, a three day week, and an oil crisis all contributing to double digit inflation, the building society movement was growing at an astonishing rate. The Leeds was no exception with its assets passing the £1 billion mark and the opening of 25 new branches that year providing real opportunities for ambitious young trainees.

When the day arrived for my visit I left the family home in Charminster Avenue, Yardley and boarded the number 11 Outer Circle bus for the two mile journey to Acocks Green. It was a grey November day but my confidence was heightened by the wearing of my new blue mac, recently acquired from the Grattans catalogue and setting me back two pounds a week. The agent was Eileen Yardley a close family friend.

My new branch was in a prime position on the Warwick Road on the same side of the street as the other societies. The local Birmingham Incorporated (BIBS) was a few doors down on one side, and the Nationwide a few doors further up on the other side. The Leeds branch was sandwiched between a cake shop (Margaret Halls) and a greengrocers (Walkers). With Greggs opposite I felt my appetite would be easily satisfied.

I entered the branch's banking hall to be greeted by a very attractive young woman who I could see was called Sue from the nameplate placed on the highly polished wooden counter in front of her. She had fashionably styled curly permed brown hair and a lovely smile. At that time there were no bandit screens and the long counter ended with two doors: one into the manager's office, the other leading to the back of the main office.
The Manager was on the phone, so Sue led me through the main office door to what would become my desk. Sitting nearby at another desk was another young woman who gave me a friendly smile. I made myself comfortable on the office chair, swiveling gently whilst chatting to the girls and waiting for my new boss to appear. It wasn't long before he stood in the doorway. I had been told at my interview that Trevor Jones was an ambitious manager in his mid-twenties. He was however of below average height, which gave me a clear view of his bald patch. He was clutching a pipe which immediately made him seem much older. I looked down at his feet expecting to see slippers but instead found a pair of highly polished brogues. My first thought was that his young age was a good sign of the prospects for very early advancement.

Actually it was my second thought as I was still appreciating Sue, the attractive cashier. Trevor introduced me to the rest of the team, by which I mean Chris Cope, the other cashier/typist who was a similar age to Sue, but with darker hair. Chris was also very friendly. I guessed that they were a little older than me. It was clear I would be the youngest member of the team at just 21 but I already felt at home and decided I was going to happy there.

LOW TECH

The following Monday I arrived for the first day of my new career. Trevor explained that my initial priority was to become a competent cashier. Due to the small number of staff everyone had to work a till at some point, even the manager. This was the case in the majority of the 400 plus Leeds branches spread across the UK.

The only technology in the branch was an electric adding machine complete with a roll of paper to print out the figures. Oh yes, there was a kettle of course, and a very small oven with a couple of heating rings. There were no computers to rely on, just your brain and the adding machine. All transactions were written on counter sheets and in customers' passbooks. I found it odd that there were no paying-in slips, only vouchers for withdrawals. This meant that if you were distracted and forgot to write the receipt on the counter pad the figures would not balance at the end of the day and there would be no way to uncover the error. It would only come to light when the customer's balance in their passbook displayed a discrepancy. Unfortunately I soon found out all about cash balances (differences). For tiny differences of less than 10p the girls introduced me to the aptly named "diddle tin". I found it most useful on more than one occasion.

The range of accounts was thankfully small. The main savings account was Paid Up Shares (PUS), a straightforward account with the only limits being a maximum investment of £10k (£20k for a joint account), and withdrawals capped at £300 for cash and £5000 for cheques. We also offered a subscription share account (Sub Shares). This was a monthly savings account with a maximum monthly amount of £32 paying an interest rate of about 1.5% above the PUS account.

A number of societies had recently introduced Term Shares, paying about 1% more than the bog-standard accounts, including our PUS. The disadvantage for customers was not being able to withdraw funds for a set period of time, often a couple of years or more. The Leeds' response was not to offer Term Shares but instead encourage customers to open both PUS and a Sub Share accounts and transfer regularly from PUS to Sub Shares. Amazingly many customers opted for this, attracted by the higher interest rate and the ability to close the accounts at any time. Consequently the Leeds' savings performance held up well for quite some time despite this competitive disadvantage.

PARTY TIME

I had only been at the branch a couple of weeks when a call came from the Regional Office, based above the Erdington branch, inviting me to a Christmas get-together at Bloomers. For readers of my first book, NotToo Bad, you will remember that this was the nightclub near The Swan. I readily accepted as I was already a fairly frequent visitor to the club, it being only 20 minutes' walk from home.

About a dozen staff from across the region met up at The Swan pub before moving over to Bloomers via the shady underpass beneath the Coventry Road (A45). The Regional Manager's secretary, Ann Lutwyche, had organised the get-together which was attended by some colleagues who travelled from the other side of the city. Living closer to the venue was Andy Bates, a management trainee/chief clerk who had joined at the Sheldon branch a couple of months before me. This was the nearest branch to Acocks Green. Andy and I were of a similar age and we hit it off straight away. We remain good friends to this day. It was a good night with plenty of dancing and the added benefit of establishing great new friends.

Back at the branch I soon settled in and found Sue particularly interesting. Apart from being very attractive, she was good fun to work with. When Trevor was out of the office attracting business support from the professional community and our admin work was done and the counter was quiet, Sue, Chris and I would find ways to amuse ourselves. Foot tig was a favourite as we got to race around on our chairs with castors zooming across the polished floor. Each till had a wooden writing slope for the counter pads on our side, with leaflet racks on the customer side providing an effective shield and enabling us to quickly halt our fun without being spotted by anyone entering the office.

One Friday about a week before Christmas our office cleaner, the wonderfully generous Mrs Edmunds, brought in a bottle of sherry. This was in addition to the usual supply of assorted chocolate bars that Mrs E presented to us each Friday evening. Sue and I decided to stay behind and attack the booze. I had never been a sherry drinker (and to this very day I can't stand the stuff) but that night I was keen to give it a go in order to get a little closer to Sue. I found out that she had recently ended her engagement and was currently unattached. The sherry slid down as easily as the chat built up. The time flew by and as the alcohol took effect I asked if she would like to come with me to the Christmas Eve party at Bloomers nightclub. Amazingly she said yes! I was elated and couldn't wait to tell my mates later that evening at the Yew Tree pub. There was however a problem. I had already bought a ticket as I was planning to go with a group of friends. When I contacted the club they informed me that all the tickets were sold but they would be selling a small number on the night. I decided to press ahead and get there early to secure Sue's ticket. This was a bit of a gamble but thankfully I managed to get one and met Sue at the entrance. Sue had driven down in her old Ford Cortina, recently bought from her uncle Jim.

The evening progressed well. We chatted easily and danced the night away. BUT when the clock struck twelve and the DJ announced the arrival of Christmas Day, I leant across the small gap between us expecting a kiss, I was met by a larger gap as Sue leant back to avoid contact. Disappointment doesn't do it justice even though I knew I was lucky to have gotten that far. This was obviously not a "date" in Sue's eyes. However, I was offered a lift home, which was only a five minute drive. As I got out of Sue's car I accidentally shut the seat belt in the door and try as I might I could not release it. This was not how I had anticipated that the night would end. Sue seemed relaxed about it all, but then drove off in the wrong direction. I was convinced that there was no future for us as a couple.

Interestingly Sue sold her Cortina to her brother Ken who somewhat bizarrely painted it with light blue emulsion paint.

THE LEEDS IS A PLACE WHERE A GIRL PUTS HER MONEY

January 1975 was the dawn of the Leeds first television advertisement. It was shown in just two television regions; ATV in the Midlands and Granada in the Northwest. Lasting 45 seconds it featured the American actress Nancy Lee dressed like Marilyn Monroe and singing the following lyrics (as far as I can remember) to the tune of Diamonds Are a Girl's Best Friend:

"The Leeds is a place where a girl puts her money if she wants to see it grow.
The Leeds is so stable the Leeds is really able, put your pound notes in and take them out without a doubt.
There's no hitch, no hidden fix, with the Leeds when you start to invest.
The Leeds is so able, the Leeds is stable, the Leeds is a girl's best friend."

Perhaps it would be judged as a little sexist by today's standards. I am not sure if it went on to appear any other region, but it was a boost for staff morale in the Midlands.

Despite the Christmas Eve set back, life in the office was still fun. On a quiet Wednesday afternoon I decided to put on a show for Sue and Chris by placing each foot into a waste paper bin and sliding up the office on the smooth tiled floor. This was great fun and very amusing until a customer came in and the girls swiftly disappeared to the back of the office out of sight. This left me staring weirdly at the customer who fortunately could not see my unusual and severely limiting footwear. I was left with no alternative but to carefully slide my feet in a way that most replicated normal walking to take up a position at my till. I just about got away with it, much to the delight of the sniggering girls.

WHAT A RELIEF

Like all new staff I had to complete a three month probationary period before being taken on to the permanent staff. Trevor had booked a week off to take his wife, Tess, and their two children down to their home town of Torquay. I was not yet eligible to sign cheques or conduct mortgage interviews so two relief staff were called in. The week was split between Bob Bayliss and Pat Moore. Bob had blond hair finished off in a confident quiff. He was nicknamed the 3Bs. I thought this was to do with the Bradford and Bingley Building Society, which was known as the 3 B's. However, I soon became aware that the middle B stood for Boring (hard but fair). Pat was much more fun. He was working at the Birmingham branch as an Area Representative. As a rep his job was to call on solicitors and banks to encourage business. This involved a fair number of lunches, which Pat obviously enjoyed, evidenced by his size. He was big in all directions. This was only temporary as he slimmed down considerably later on.

INDUCTION

After just six weeks I was off up to Head Office in Leeds for my induction course. Fortunately, I was offered a lift by Andy from Sheldon branch who I had met at the Bloomers "do" a few weeks earlier. Another local trainee, Dan Heaphy was also on the same course. Apparently, Dan had answered the same advert as me and was still at the main Birmingham office, about to transfer to a Chief Clerk position. On the Sunday afternoon Andy and I headed north in his impressive Ford Escort feeling both excited and somewhat apprehensive as we readied ourselves to enter the unknown.

About a dozen newly recruited trainees were on the course designed to open our eyes to life with the Leeds. We all stayed at the comfortable Merrion Hotel, which was within walking distance of Permanent House, the Leeds headquarters located on the Headrow.

Andy was a year younger than Dan and I and we were surprised that a couple of the other chaps on the course were considerably older. Mike Bown for instance was chief clerk at Bridgewater branch in Somerset. He had joined from the local Bridgewater Building Society and brought his Somerset twang with him. Mike was close to forty but didn't look it. He was friendly with a good sense of humour and not quite a Wurzel. I would get to know Mike really well in the future. This was 1975 and at this time there were no female branch managers or even female management trainees but the times they were a changing!

There were presentations from the managers of the main departments such as Investment, Securities, Insurance and Advance (Mortgages). The talks varied in quality and ability to hold our attention, due mainly to the competence of the presenter. The most interesting session was when the training department played a couple of films featuring John Cleese and Tim Brooke Taylor. They made fun of the way managers behaved, and it was a memorable way of showing what NOT to do. We also had a guided tour of the building and were shown the new tower block (Albion House) that was taking shape and would be opened in a few months' time, adding vital additional space for the expanding business.

In the middle of the week a private room was booked at our hotel where some of the senior management joined us for an evening meal. General Manager Arthur Stone and Assistant General Manager Ted Germaine circulated the room ensuring that they spoke to us all at some point. They were complete opposites. Arthur was in his mid-forties with little hair and a serious demeanour. He told me in a very downbeat manner how disappointing the investment figures were at my branch. He had expected much more from us now that we had been open for a couple of years. Ted was younger, in his thirties and very positive. His thinning hair and slightly too many teeth didn't detract from his flamboyant nature, helped by the colourful handkerchief neatly escaping from his breast pocket. He seemed genuinely interested in each and every one of us. He painted a very positive picture of the future for the business and our potential place in its success.

Andy, Dan and I made the most of the evenings, venturing out to Cinderella Rockefellers the popular nightclub just around the corner from our hotel. We mixed with the stars, well one of them. We spotted the Leeds United centre half Gordon McQueen in there. The 6'3" footballer stood out amongst the crowd and attracted an ever-present following of young ladies. The three of us tried to stretch ourselves to greater heights but were sadly unable to build any sort of following.

On the last day we finished at lunchtime and crossed the Headrow to the Guildford pub for a couple of drinks with the boys and one or two of the presenters. It had been a very enjoyable week. It was particularly good to get to know other trainees and understand more about the Leeds and its role within the wider financial services industry.

PROBATION ENDED

Trevor took great delight in being as slow as possible to confirm that I had made enough progress to be officially added to the permanent staff. It was not all good news as I also joined the contributory pension scheme. The financial implications of joining were short lived as the rapid rise in the cost of living led to a 10% pay increase for all staff. Before the year was out another 10% rise was implemented as inflation soared. This was not good news for the economy but as a young single lad living at home it was more than welcome.

Fred Chaffer, the Regional Manager, paid a visit and officially welcomed me as a member of permanent staff. Sadly, it was the last time I saw him as his trademark persistent cough turned out to serious and he passed away shortly afterwards. Norman Weatherhead, the Birmingham Branch Manager who recruited me, was appointed as Fred's replacement. He was a popular choice. Still in his thirties and a keen cricketer, he was well liked by everyone. Norman was quickly nicknamed "Spiny Norman" after the Monty Python character. To be fair the only thing he had in common with the giant hedgehog was his name.

'Spiny' was an excellent communicator and very keen to encourage us trainees. He sat and passed the Chartered Building Societies Institute Associateship examinations and actively encouraged us to follow suit. There were six papers to pass with some subjects being compulsory. In my last year at the solicitors I had completed the final one of the four Legal Executive papers to become an Associate of the Institute of Legal Executives but was still keen to follow Spiny's example. The difference was the only college support was in the city centre and travelling in and out would have proven difficult so I considered a correspondence course. I received all the details from Rapid Results but found the prospect daunting to say the least. It didn't look rapid to me and I put the papers back in the envelope and my ambition on the back burner, actually more like inside the fridge!

NOT SO GREEN

Many interesting customers visited us at The Green. One of our regular favourites was Mr Green (real name). He was a retired accountant who was clearly wealthy, as evidenced by his regular deposits. He lived at home with his mother. We never saw her but she was mentioned on every visit, a bit like Mainwaring's wife in Dad's Army. He wore the same beige mac in all weathers. It had clearly seen better days, but then so had he. He was severely follicly challenged and had one eye that we were sure was not an original, but we loved him.

Barely a week went by without Mr G presenting his PUS passbook stuffed with dividend cheques. He told us how much he loved coming into our branch. He was always cheerful and pleasant. He repeatedly told us that he had most of his money elsewhere but preferred to come to us with all his regular transaction because of the way we had befriended him.

On day Mr G took me to one side and advised me, very earnestly to invest as much as I possibly could in the stock market. At the time the all-share index was at an all time low of less than 100, compared to todays' figure of 4000 (2018). He made the point that he had many shares in all sorts of companies, as was clear from the vast number of dividend cheques he paid in. "It has to recover and you can make a fortune along with me" he said confidently. My total wealth at the time would have probably bought me a suit, or maybe two, and there was my debt to Grattans for my mac to consider. I thanked him for his advice and explained my lack of available funds. He continued to be a regular favourite customer but steadfastly refused to move his big investments over to us, despite our best efforts.

Being a high street branch, from time to time we received some very strange requests from passers-by. Unlike banks we had large window spaces we used to promote our products on "show cards". One popular show card featured an attractive young lady dressed in a leotard. She was pictured in a yoga position with her legs entwined. I think the caption was something to do with not letting your savings get wrapped up. One day a chap wondered in off the street and asked us to save it for him after the display period ended. As you would expect we tactfully declined his strange request. I was told later that the young lady was Josie Holden who worked for the Society in Leeds. I am not sure if it was Josie and have never raised the subject since. I wonder how many of those show cards went astray and how many are still propped up in back rooms up and down the country!

STEPPING UP THE WORK

As a relatively small branch we only had a modest allocation of mortgage funds. This meant we could only process one or perhaps two mortgages a week. Demand was strong from both customers and professional connections. This led to a waiting list that could extend to several weeks. Back then there were jokes on TV such as a customer asking, "How do I stand for a mortgage?" Answer, "You don't, you kneel and beg!" Priority was carefully given to our regular savers wherever possible.

The bulk of the processing and decision-making was carried out at Head Office. Each application was completed at the branch and the income references and property valuation obtained. These were then sent in the Envopak with other Head Office post to the Mortgage Advance Department. Unless there were any queries, a mortgage offer would be sent out along with instructions to the customer's solicitors, who also acted for the Society. This seemingly straightforward process became more localised in time.

There were two main types of mortgage, standard rate and endowment. The latter had a higher rate of 0.5% above the standard rate due to there being no repayment of the loan until the life (endowment) policy matured. The staff rate was 3%, being way below the public rate of around 11%. Tax relief was also available which made a mortgage application an extremely attractive proposition for all staff, but I was keen to save for a deposit towards a decent car and was comfortable at home.

DRIVEN TO DISTRACTION

Another attractive benefit offered by The Leeds was the provision of a company car for all branch managers. Trevor had a Hillman Avenger which was changed every year. Its business use was mostly limited to visiting professional connections and arrears calls. Trevor would make regular visits to our agents at Hall Green who acted as a mini branch but with limited cash facilities and were often more trouble than they were worth due to lack of knowledge and many cashiering errors.

Having watched Trevor for a few months, it struck me that the life of a building society branch manager was a bit of a doddle. A typical day would see him arrive just before 9am. Sue or Chris would either open the post or make the first round of milky coffee whilst Trevor read the office copy of the Telegraph. He would then go through the few items that were left after the girls had removed the standard post. These would then be passed to me with any necessary instructions. His pipe was then filled, tapped and puffed. I can still smell the aroma of the Benson and Hedges ready-rubbed that I was so often instructed to purchase for him from Preedys, the newsagents across the road.

After his second cup of coffee Trevor would leave the office perhaps to carry out an arrears call requested by HO. More often than not there would be no one at home and he would leave his calling card asking the owners to contact the branch. I soon learnt that managers were advised to be ex-directory to avoid getting angry calls to their homes.

A couple of times a week Trevor would have lunch with a solicitor or other professional contact. This would nearly always involve the odd drink, or two, which would lead to some entertainment for the rest of us on his return. On one occasion, when he had rather more than two drinks, Sue and Chris decided to secure him to his chair once he had nodded off. As they stepped back to admire their handiwork a phone call came in for Trevor. Sue took great delight in telling the caller that the manager was a bit tied up at the moment!

Trevor's final duty of the day was signing the outgoing post before locking up and heading home. From what I could tell it was certainly an easy life but I was not totally convinced that at this stage, it was the life for me. At Wragge and Co Solicitors I had been used to often quite challenging work requiring research and careful consideration. Although I enjoyed working at The Leeds I wasn't sure that I wanted to settle for Trevor's professional lifestyle.

SECURITY, WHAT SECURITY?

Robberies were rare at Leeds branches, which was pretty surprising given the lack of security. There were no screens, alarms or panic buttons. We didn't hold very much cash which led to frequent unaccompanied trips to the bank to either deposit the daily takings or exchange a branch cheque for cash if we were running low. Lloyds Bank was just over the road, close to Preedys, which meant I could pick up Trevor's ready-rubbed on the way back. Quite often I would return to the branch with two or three thousand pounds in my pocket without a second thought.

We were briefed regularly on the need to be on the lookout for suspicious packages either sent through the post or left in the banking hall. The week I left Wragge & Co the Birmingham pub bombings had taken place meaning we were all very aware of the current risks.

One quiet afternoon when Trevor was out of the office one of the girls noticed a brief case on the floor in the empty banking hall. What were we to do? I took charge and following our standard instructions, vacated the premises with Sue and Chris, and phoned both the police and HO. The police arrived in minutes…. at about the same time as the customer who was running back to retrieve his briefcase! He was most apologetic and obviously relieved his belongings were intact. The police informed me that I had done everything right EXCEPT it probably wasn't a good idea to all lean against the outside wall only a few yards from a potential bomb. Lesson learnt.

In other ways our wellbeing was secured by the monthly appearance of the telephone cleaning lady. She would spray and disinfect each phone throughout the branch. The treatment only worked on certain types of bugs, certainly not the hacking kind! It was a bizarre waste of money. Our other health benefit was a subscription to the Leeds Hospital Fund that paid out to help with dental, optical and other medical costs. I am not sure if it covered the treatment of infections caused by unhygienic telephones. Any such claim may have been a close call.

OUT THE DOOR

Building societies had a distinct advantage over the clearing banks by opening until midday on a Saturday morning. This was the busiest period of the week with customers queuing sometimes out on to the street. We always had all three tills open and one of us would have to lock the doors at noon, trapping prompt customers inside and tactfully refusing entry to late arrivals. Our pay was double time for Saturdays, which meant I was always keen to help out, particularly as I still had time to play football for Wylde Green in the afternoon.

Other than Saturdays the busiest periods were at the end of March and September when savings interest was paid. A statement slip would be posted out from HO for every account stating the amount credited to the account and the new balance. The credit was automatic meaning that no action was required, as the passbook would be made up to date on the next visit to the branch. This did not stop customers coming in their droves as soon as the statement arrived through their letterbox. All we did was stamp the date (31st March or 30th September) and update the balance. The queues were always enormous in all Leeds branches across the country.

Customers could alternatively opt for a cheque for the interest to be sent with the statement (known as a warrant). A large number of those who requested to have their interest to be paid out would turn up to immediately pay the cheque back in. Very odd indeed.

ROOM FOR STAFF

When I was working at Wragge & Co I developed a reputation for being able to easily acquire decent office furniture and equipment. Upstairs at Acocks Green we had a small kitchen and toilets. In addition there was a large room that was full of unwanted materials, including old window displays (not the yoga girl!) and a box of Christmas decorations. I asked Trevor if we could use it as a staff room. He agreed, and we soon installed an old three-piece suite that was no longer needed by Sue's brother Ken. Fortunately, it hadn't suffered the same fate as the emulsioned Ford Cortina. My brother Steve gave us an old carpet and I brought in an old TV set. It was a real home from home, and importantly somewhere comfortable for me to eat my cheese and tomato cobs from Greggs across the road and for Sue to polish off yet another individual trifle from Margaret Hall's next door. The only problem was the TV. It was old and only showed ITV and BBC in black and white but we had become quite attached to it. The real problem was Trevor's insistence that we paid for a TV licence. He was quite right and despite grumbling we eventually pooled resources and were all set. Sad person that I am I began to watch Emmerdale Farm on a regular basis at lunchtime. Its title included the word 'Farm' and there were no plane crashes or murders, just the everyday story of country folk but with the Sugdens replacing the Archers.

JUST GOOD FRIENDS

Sue and I continued to get on well and enjoy each other's company. There were one or two events away from the branch where we had good fun. The Leeds was keen to reward good performance and Spiny Norman supported all branch managers to take their teams out for a nice meal if the investment receipts beat the previous high. The branch performance was improving and one record month for investment receipts encouraged Trevor to take the four of us out at the Society's expense for a very nice evening meal at the Plough on the Stratford Road. We all got on as the wine flowed and we all relaxed.

Sue was a popular girl and was asked out by several chaps who regularly popped into the branch. By this time I had written off my chances of becoming more than friends and had reluctantly settled for foot tig and playing with a neatly constructed ball of rubber bands, at quiet times only of course. Directly opposite the branch was the stop for the number 44 bus. This meant that on the odd occasion we could be viewed over the window back by the bus passengers sat upstairs. Sue's Mum was a regular on the route and reported a few strange "goings on" from her vantage point. Probably no more than a bit of foot tig.

On Wednesday afternoons "The Green" was very quiet as most of the shops had half day closing. Trevor was kind enough to let one of us leave early if the work was up to date, which it nearly always was. We gratefully took it in turns to accept this kind offer, which sometimes enabled a full half-day to be enjoyed.

To speed up my savings towards a car I asked for permission to take a part time evening bar job at my local pub the Ring O' Bells (known to us as The Ringers) in Church Road, Yardley. Trevor knew it would only be for a couple of months until I had enough for a deposit and gave his permission as long as it did not affect my work. My good friend Terry Twinberrow was already working behind the bar in addition to his full time job at Tofts the butchers at the Yew Tree.

I had been at The Ringers for a few weeks when one night I was pleasantly surprised when two familiar faces appeared. It was Sue and Chris who had decided to see what I was up to at my local. The next day they gave me some stick over my attire. I thought I looked pretty cool in my favourite jeans - a pair of light blue denim flares with a rather colourful embroided scene featuring American football on my rear. I was of course somewhat flattered that their attention had been drawn in that direction!

In the middle of the summer Terry and I decided to take a break from our pub duties and set off in his orange minivan to stay with his sister Ann and her husband Roger on the Isle of Wight. After a few days we moved on to Braunton in North Devon to stay at Terry's uncle's pub, The George. There I met a lovely girl called Frankie who had relocated there for the summer season in order to get over her cancelled wedding. Frankie was Terry's cousin and lived with her parents in Wythall only a couple of miles from me. We got on well and promised to keep in touch and meet up when the season was over. By the time we met up on her return in October I had purchased a metallic turquoise Hillman Imp. I was excited by Frankie's arrival, particularly as Sue was now definitely in the "just good friends" category. Sue was indeed a good friend and even helped me buy Frankie's Christmas present. At the same time Sue's latest date put her well out of my reach. Sadly, Frankie and I were frankly not on quite the same wavelength for very long and I was back on my own as we entered 1976.

NOT SO DUMB

A new year and a new dawn on the technology front. The IBM 3600 had arrived with a promise to improve customer service. It was called a 'dumb terminal' because it had no local intelligence, so it was not really a computer as such. What it could do was add up the counter sheets and speed up the end of day balancing. It also enabled you to view a customer's balance in their account. The big bonus for HO was substantial staff savings as all the data entry was now performed at branch level without the need for extra staff.

INTROS AND OUTROS

There weren't many professional contacts in our area. The brokers J. Hall were our agents (mini branches) at Hall Green; and Edwards Properties became agents on Fox Hollies Road. There were one or two solicitors' firms but the scope for Trevor to obtain new business was limited.

One of Trevor's mortgage contacts was a real character. Gerry Higginbotham was a mortgage broker who had an office in Sparkhill. He was a large chap in his thirties with big glasses and an Irish accent. He was known to be the life and soul of the party and popped in regularly for the "craic". I bumped into Gerry occasionally in the local pubs and he always insisted on buying the drinks. He also introduced investment funds as well as mortgages. Never pushy and always smiling, he was a great favourite and always welcome.

WHAT A RELIEF

If local branches found themselves short staffed, due to holidays or sickness we were always keen to help each other out. The two branches nearest to The Green were Sheldon and Solihull. The manager at Sheldon was Tim Battell, a Londoner who had strayed north. In his early thirties he struck me as a bit of a barrow boy. His Chief Clerk was my friend Andy Bates. I helped out there a couple of times. It was a well run branch and it was easy for me to fit in. The same could not be said of all branches. Ken McMullen managed the Solihull branch. He had opened Acocks Green before being promoted to the posh end of town. The Chief Clerk there was so thin and pale that someone once very unkindly said he thought he was the only man to survive a post-mortem! The two cashier typists were Heather and Lydia. Ken was from Northern Ireland, in his thirties and balding. He was great fun and ever cheerful. The Chief Clerk's personality matched his complexion. Heather had a strong personality with a deep voice to match. It was a smoker's voice even though I don't think she had ever actually lit a cigarette. Lydia was a very pleasant young girl who had only recently joined when I went on relief.

Solihull sounded like it should have been a great place to work but it was actually in total chaos. There should have been a signature card for each account, filed in alphabetical order, to enable customer verification particularly for withdrawals. There were none. The team had made a decision not to bother filing them, which meant no checking. This was of course a high risk strategy.

When Lydia was recruited as a shorthand typist cashier it was overlooked that she had no shorthand and could not type. Ken told me Lydia's 'other assets' more than made up for this! Suffice it to say, once you had been there you tried not to go

24

back. Lovely people, but it was an unsettling experience to say the least.

DEVELOPMENTS

As winter turned to spring things started to develop. I had talked to Spiny, my Regional Manager, revealing my frustration at not making any progress with my exams. I had discovered that you could sign up for a full-time course to polish most of them off but this would mean taking leave for a few months. Spiny was sympathetic but could not support my leave of absence, as he felt this would set a difficult precedent. He encouraged me to stay as he intended to move me to the large Birmingham branch (Temple Row) for further training. From here I could attend day release at Matthew Boulton College where I had previously studied for the Legal Executive exams. I decided this was a good option and waited for the call.

Chris Cope had now become Chris Lees following her marriage to long term boyfriend Terry. They lived in a flat only a few hundred yards from the branch. Terry was a busy disc jockey who was often accompanied to his work by Chris. Sue and I were getting closer and when Trevor asked Sue what she was looking for in a man he reported back that her description sounded like Dumb, Dumb Duffin (as he often called me). Soon after this revelation Sue and I went to one of Terry's gigs at Sloopys nightclub in the city centre. As Terry ended his session with 10cc's "I'm not in love" Sue and I were as one, but we didn't tell Trevor for a few weeks. When we thought it was appropriate we told Trevor of our relationship. We need not have worried, as he seemed genuinely pleased for us.

Not long after this the call came from Spiny confirming my move to Temple Row for "further training". On the whole I had enjoyed my 18 months at The Green but was eager to progress. I had learnt the basics of cashiering including knowledge of all the products. I had been exposed to how a manager runs a branch and motivates a team. Day release was now a real attraction, and I felt it would be better for our new relationship if Sue and I worked at separate branches.

CHAPTER 2
BIRMINGHAM TEMPLE ROW
MAY 1976 TO OCTOBER 1977

IN THE CHURCHYARD

My new branch was located on Temple Row in the very heart of the city. Facing out on to St Philip's cathedral its open churchyard was an oasis of green amidst the built up cityscape.

St. Phillip's was built at the beginning of the 18th century in the Baroque style and is the third smallest cathedral in England. It was consecrated in 1715 as a small parish church but became a cathedral in 1905 with the formation of the new Diocese of Birmingham. It was severely damaged by German bombs in November 1940 but fortunately the treasured stained glass windows had been taken to safety when war broke out and were replaced, unharmed when hostilities ceased.

BIG BRANCH

Temple Row was one of the largest Leeds branches both in terms of its physical size and the business conducted. There was a rudimentary branch grading system which divided more than 400 branches into grades 9,10 and 11, with 11 being the highest grade but featuring the fewest branches. Temple Row was a highly ranked grade 11 branch. Senior managers saw it as an important stepping-stone to regional management.

It was physically imposing with a large banking hall with six tills positioned along the long polished wooden counter. The main hall faced square-on to the huge front window, providing a perfect opportunity to display a long row of show cards advertising Leeds products. On entering the branch there were two interview rooms on the left hand side. Of those, the one to the right was also home to the Chief Clerk, Glyn (Knocker) Powell.

He had been with the Leeds for many years most of which were spent at the branch in his hometown of Wolverhampton. His roots were evidenced by his strong Black Country accent, which was markedly different to my Brummie twang. In his early forties with glasses and thinning hair he was straightforward and pleasant enough. I think the name "Knocker" probably came from Enoch Powell, the controversial Tory MP. Like a number of chief clerks he was happy to stay at his current level rather than move his family around the country as this often meant a spouse would be forced to leave a very good career behind.

On arrival I was welcomed by Glyn at the "wicket" gate at the end of the counter and taken into his adjacent office. He took me through some of the basic office routines such as lunch rotas, Saturday morning allocation and asked me to sign the cheque signing forms. He went on to briefly explain the way work was divided between trainees and wished me well.

ALEXANDER THE GREAT?

Glyn had just about finished explaining till rotation when the manager Harvey Alexander entered the room. His southern accent was unusual as London managers rarely ventured as far north as Birmingham. Harvey was obviously seen as having the potential for regional management. He was in his thirties, of average height with a Bobby Charlton combover hiding his thinning hair. He was very welcoming and seemed to want to see the trainees move quickly through his domain.

Harvey quickly disappeared into his office, which was situated about twenty yards deeper into the back office area. I seldom saw him again. The only time I spent with him was at my annual appraisal that wasn't due for a few months.

THE SET UP

Apart from Temple Row there were seven other Leeds branches in the Birmingham suburbs. This saturation had led to a substantial build up of business with many customers using both their local branch and Temple Row. The counter was always busy and needed four full-time cashiers who were then supported by the rest of the staff with a few exceptions, including Harvey, the two reps and the chief clerk.

Joy led the counter girls. Tall with strawberry blonde hair she was strongly built and could scare us trainees to death. However, Joy was extremely efficient and once she had confidence in your cashiering ability, provided great support. Her commanding voice was readily obeyed by all, including the customers. When necessary she could shift a whole queue to a fresh till in moments.

Eileen was less imposing than Joy but no less efficient. With interesting Irish eyes she was as straight as a die with a fun side. She did not stand any nonsense and was always great with customers. Margaret was as sweet as they come. She could have been mistaken for being Spanish or Italian with characteristic dark hair and attractive features. Finally, there was Cathy who was tall, dark, with striking looks. She was the newest and youngest of the four but soon became a valued part of a great team.

OVERRUN WITH TRAINEES

Glyn escorted me from his office to the open office area where there were four standard issue Leeds desks arranged two by two facing each other. This was to be my new workstation. I was delighted to see my friend Andy Bates sitting at one of the desks. He had recently moved from the Sheldon branch. Due to the rapid expansion of the branch network it was necessary to recruit and train a significant number of trainees so he was not alone. Few branches could cater for such an influx of 'newbies' but Birmingham Temple Row was an exception.

Sitting around the four desks were Mike Mitchell, Dave Hartle, Dave Shuttleworth and of course Andy. I was positioned next to Andy and informed that this was known as "middle desk", which looked after anything to do with existing mortgages such as additional loans for home improvements and repayment arrears. Mike was of slim build with dark hair and a fairly threadbare moustache to match. Having already been a chief clerk he was in a similar position to Andy and me. He was given responsibility for new mortgages and took his job very seriously. It was clear that Glyn and Harvey relied heavily on him, but he had a good sense of humour and was great to work alongside.

Dave Hartle was a real character. Strongly built with wavy hair he was always wisecracking and making us laugh. As a fellow Villa fan from my side of town we quickly bonded.

Dave S was the odd one out. He was a real enigma as he had arrived unannounced from the Coventry branch where he had been Chief Clerk for a while. He wore a rather dated three-piece suit frequently accompanied by a patterned shirt. His long fair hair was matched with long side burns. Most days he could have passed for Worzel Gummidge's love child! He kept himself to himself and appeared to do very little, sat on his own at the end desk.

I sat in my place alongside Andy and began to settle in.

LESLIE JONES'S LOCKER

All the trainees took it in turns to make the drinks in the kitchen downstairs. The mugs were carried back up to our desks using an extra long ruler pushed through all of the handles. Andy was always worried about slopping the contents and became so careful with this task that he only partially filled each mug. He was soon christened "half cup Bates".

Sometime during my first week as I sat drinking my coffee I noticed the other lads delving in the bottom drawer of one of the filing cabinets next to Glyn's office, each returning with a bag of crisps. I asked if they were available to all and was soon munching away with the rest of them at each break. It took the lads until the end of the week to inform me with great delight that I had accrued quite a debt and would have to settle up with Les Jones.

Les was a rotund chap in his fifties. Being very proud of his army service he always wore his regimental tie. Even so you could not describe Les as "well turned out". He wore the same old suit with a similarly crumpled shirt every day, and his tie bore evidence of past lunches at the often frequented nearby Windsor pub.

When not at The Windsor he could be found at his desk nestled in a space at the top of the stairs that led down to the kitchen. This was particularly handy for his frequent visits to the facilities down below. If you met him as he was rushing down the narrow stairs he would mutter, "Sorry Paul can't stop, terrible problem, diarrhoea".

Apparently Les came with the building many years back and was originally employed as an Area Representative but unfortunately this role didn't suit him. He was retained to perform what could only be described as basic tasks. These included updating the mortgage register and completing reference cards for each mortgage application. He seemed to particularly enjoy underlining, with very few words or names avoiding his red pen and ruler. He did however provide us with one vital service: "the tuck shop".

Les owned a newsagents shop on the Stratford Road, which was mainly run by his wife Connie while he was at the branch. In addition to the crisps in the filing cabinet, Les stocked two of his desk drawers with an array of chocolate bars. All sorts could be found including Kit Kats, Crunchies and Mars bars. You helped yourself and put the money in the sliding drawer section designed to hold pens and pencils. You could also ask for a tab for which no details were ever kept, and therefore relied solely on your memory and honesty. The system worked well until Les went on holiday forcing us to consume bars that had lurked at the bottom of the drawers for who knows how long. From time to time some of the crisp packets became punctured and Les was then open to negotiation on the price. There were occasional suspicions that some jiggery-pokery had been committed, enabling deflation of the crisp packet and consequently its price.

OUT BACK

At the end of the corridor that went past Harvey's office was the typing area. This housed five girls and seemed to be run by Gill who was probably the most senior in age and authority. A bit like Joy, you were well advised to stay on her right side but really she was fine when you got to know her. Her husband was a fireman and it was rumoured that his fire axe was in her bottom drawer, but I am sure this was a myth.

It soon became clear that there was a certain amount of rivalry between the counter girls and the back office team. Being on the counter meant there was no hiding place and you were on your feet all day. The girls in the back office received less scrutiny and felt less pressure. During busy periods they were called to work on the counter, which they were less than keen on and this caused occasional disputes. We were literally in the middle and forced to mediate over which team was the busier.

Jackie acted as Harvey's PA and could also claim to run the back office. With dark hair and a walk that attracted the lads' attention, she was efficient and helpful, especially to Mike! Our office junior, the fair-haired Angela, was employed to answer the phone and carry out basic office tasks as well as learning shorthand typing. She had confidence beyond her years and soon shed her "junior" tag.

Apart from Gill the two main typists were Lynn and Bev. They would appear together at our desks each morning for dictation. Much of this time was spent just chatting with banter flowing around the desks. Lynn had short blonde hair and a pretty smile. She was married to a milkman, who she referred to as "Mickey the milk". We learnt that they had a cat appropriately named "Gold Top". One day Lynn appeared for dictation clearly upset. She explained that there was a problem with the cat. What has happened we enquired? "Gold Top has just gone off!" she blurted out. Naturally we burst into fits of laughter. Lynn was not amused at first but came round later. I am not sure Gold Top did. It was reported that a cat, fitting Gold Top's description had been discovered in a chemist shop near Lynn's home. However, it turned out there was no truth in the rumour that there had been a Puss in Boots! (Sorry about that I just couldn't resist it).

Both Lynn and Bev were competent at shorthand with good speeds. Bev always seemed a bit different to the other girls. Quite petite with short darkish hair, Andy called her "little Bev, the forces favourite". She was quietly spoken and just got on with her work.

Angela, the office junior, was gradually being encouraged to develop her growing shorthand skills by braving dictation from the trainees. Her shorthand speed was slowly increasing but one day she just couldn't keep up with Andy's rapid pace. Not being one to hold back she firmly told Andy to slow down. Being his usual playful self, Andy slowed to a crawl and began dictating a letter to a customer with "thank you for your extremely slow letter dated 6th June....". Seemingly unnoticed by Angela he went on to include the words "extremely slow" throughout. When Angela brought the post for signature later that afternoon she had typed the letter exactly as Andy had dictated it. After the laughter had died down Angela produced the proper version for Andy to sign.

Next day the phone rang and we heard Andy apologising profusely to the caller. The wrong copy had been sent out to our valuer at Dixon Dobson and Carver. Andy saw the funny side of it and fortunately so did the caller. Angela claimed she had not sent it out deliberately. We may never know.

This was not the only trick that was played on us trainees. It happened to me one day when Joy came over to my desk and asked me to see a customer who wanted to discuss a serious investment. I took the gentleman into the interview room and settled him down and asked how I could help. His reply was a little confusing. He produced a notebook and opened it on the desk. He began to speak; "Bin here, bin there, bin there, bin here...". As he spoke he flicked through the pages of his notebook. All I could see were date stamps from various institutions around town. I tried to find out more but he simply repeated his lines. I left the office feeling bemused only to discover a group of sniggering staff. Joy came over with a date stamp in her hand and told me he was a regular visitor to the branch who really just wanted a stamp in his book. I duly carried out the stamping and he left the branch smiling. Apparently, I was not the first to be" had" and I certainly wasn't the last.

AREA REPRESENTATIVES

Due to the large number of professional local firms offering potential business, Temple Row had two reps at any one time although they didn't usually stay long before becoming full branch managers. It would usually only be a matter of months before they received a letter from HO in a pink envelope telling them of their branch management appointment. The reps that summer were Bill Mackrill and Geoff Perkins. Bill was a little above average height with dark hair and matching moustache. He had a confident air and looked the part. Geoff was a little shorter with wavy fair hair and a well-fed body. They had desks opposite each other and not far from us trainees. Being reps they disappeared for most of the day as they walked around the city centre calling on banks, solicitors and other professional contacts. Their Hillman Imp company cars were rarely used for business except when they were needed for taking contacts to lunch at venues outside the city centre. Their favourite restaurant was in the basement of the Waterloo, an Edwardian pub frequented by many of the city's professional community. The basement grillroom was famous for its tiled walls and ceiling. It had an excellent reputation for steaks and puddings, complemented by renowned cask ales.

Part of our further training was to learn from the reps how to master their role and thus smooth our transition upwards. There was an unwritten rule that as a rep you made about seven calls (visits to professionals) each day. This was to ensure consistency when your weekly expenses sheet detailing the calls you had made was signed off by the manager. I am not sure Harvey ever questioned anything but the understanding seemed to be pretty consistent across the country. There were so many professional contacts found in the Waterloo pub that we speculated that on occasions all seven "calls" could be achieved in a single lunchtime.

COLLEGE BOYS

There was good news on the exam front. The timing was perfect for us to sign up at Matthew Boulton College to study for three of the exams starting a couple of months later in September. Harvey readily agreed to sponsor Andy, Mike and myself to have half-day release on a Tuesday to attend the afternoon economics lecture. In the evening there were classes covering building society management and building society development and marketing.

We became friendly with another student at the college, a lad called Andrew Caunce who was a trainee at the Woolwich Building society in the city centre. The economics lecturer was Dr White who bore a striking resemblance to the ventriloquist Ray Alan, although there was no sign of Lord Charles. He was a permanent member of staff at the college and a capable lecturer. The evening lecturers were building society managers who worked part-time as lecturers. Bill Clee took us for marketing and had a real liking for the word "folks". He used it so often that we soon began to keep score. At least it forced us to concentrate as we regularly became a little weary towards the end of the evening sessions.

Parts of the economics course were interesting but we spent the whole of the three months from September to the Christmas break studying National Income. Not the most exciting subject, but what was infuriating was that not one question on the topic appeared in the May examination. The boys were not impressed having spent a substantial amount of time studying it. When we complained to Dr White his only response was: "Don't worry you can come back and do the course again in September". The good news was that when the results came out we had all passed all three subjects. A great start meant we could take the remaining three subjects at our own pace.

There were some evenings when we skived off early and missed a lecture or two. The attraction of the nearby Trees pub, on the Bristol Road, was sometimes just too tempting. Our attendance record was sent direct to Harvey clearly showing any missed sessions, but he was kindly silent on the subject.

There was however one college related incident that has since come back to haunt me. On leaving college one Tuesday evening it was pouring with rain and the roads were suffering under the deluge. I was giving the lads a lift home in my Hillman Imp (my own not the Leeds). We dived into the car for cover and I quickly turned the ignition key. Nothing, no reassuring click, no roar of the engine, it was as dead as a dodo. My knowledge of car mechanics was never strong and as everything about me was soaked I confidently declared that the problem must be due to a wet ignition key. The laughter was deafening and lasted a long time. I have been frequently reminded of this outrageous claim. There was however some retribution, as when the laughing stopped but the downpour continued, the lads had to get out and push.

FANHAMS HALL WELL AND GOOD

The previous year I was pleased to discover that the Building Society Institute had a very professional training centre situated in Ware, Hertfordshire. Fanhams Hall was built at the beginning of the 18th century and remained a country house until the Westminster Bank acquired it as a training centre in 1951. The Building Society Institute subsequently purchased it from them in 1971.

I had first experienced the lovely country house atmosphere of Fanhams when I attended a general introductory course whilst working at Acocks Green. Accommodation was shared but comfortable. The food was excellent and the well-stocked bar was amusingly run by Rodney, an extremely camp barman. The work was never too taxing which always led to an enjoyable stay.

Our forthcoming exams meant that Andy, Mike and I were able to return to the Hall for a three-day exam refresher course. These were intense sessions but well worth the effort and proved invaluable preparation for the exams. Lots of very helpful "crib sheets" were handed out to help with revision. We would return for more help in the future.

ON YOUR MARKS

Appraisal time soon came round and I felt pretty confident that I had made sufficient progress to impress Harvey. There was a standard Leeds appraisal form with each category containing tick boxes for four levels. Next to each level there was space for additional comments to support the level awarded. I was warned by my fellow trainees to expect a surprise.

It was more like a shock as Harvey worked his way methodically through the form awarding me the top level for each category. I could not believe it but chose not to challenge the obvious accuracy of Harvey's assessment. The trouble was he had given us all the same marks. His decision to give us trainees a very easy ride meant that he could spend most of his time with the two area reps and outside contacts, frequently at The Waterloo.

A CLOSE SHAVE

The throughput of trainees and reps was relentless with new trainees appearing regularly. Chris Dix soon joined us putting the four desks space under pressure. Chris had a strong southern accent that made Harvey sound almost posh. I think he had moved up to the Midlands as his partner Liz was from the area. Chris was a victim of one of the Leeds strangest policies, no beards. Chris found this out when he appeared fully fuzzed at his interview. He was promptly told to shave it off before being allowed across the threshold. The reason given was 'customer acceptance' although a more interesting hypothesis was that someone in senior management was unable to grow one. It was not just the men that were restricted by the rules, as the ladies had not been allowed to wear trousers for some time.

Moustaches were in fashion and most of the lads wore them, including Mike, Andy and me. For some of us it took a while to reach maximum hair density in the key area. I had previously suffered a series of boils on my back and big toe so was deeply shocked to discover a boil developing in the midst of my moustache. I immediately rushed to consult my GP and joined the seated queue that shuffled from seat to seat towards the doctor's room. When my turn came I was in and out in a flash clutching a prescription for antibiotics. Would early intervention save my precious 'tache? No, not a chance! Within a couple of days I was losing the battle with an obvious bald patch beginning to take shape under my nose. The office banter began and I was soon reaching for my electric shaver. After a week or so the boil had gone but so had my 'tache. It grew back eventually but it seemed to take a long time and looked a bit of a mess for a while.

ONWARDS AND UPWARDS

The two reps, Bill and Geoff were soon on the move, but they didn't get very far. Their pink envelopes took them to branches in the Birmingham suburbs: Bill to Kings Heath and Geoff to my old branch at Acocks Green. My old boss Trevor Jones had been desperate to take his family back as close to Torquay as possible. He was not totally happy to now be moved many miles south to Newport in South Wales as he was still a long way from Torquay. I was convinced his surname had some bearing on his welsh destination.

Away from work things were going well with Sue although she was beginning to feel unsettled by the many changes taking place at the Acocks Green branch. After I left the replacement chief clerk was David Bramwell. David was old-school in most respects. As one pipe smoker left (Trevor) another one (David) arrived. Of average height and build, with glasses and an oversupply of teeth David could pass for many years older than his late twenties. With Geoff arriving to replace Trevor the branch developed a very different atmosphere. Fortunately, Chris and Sue were still there to help keep things on an even keel. Sue knew a lot of the Leeds staff in the area and came to most of the social events that we had at Birmingham. As a couple we would also meet up with Andy and his girlfriend, also called Sue.

On my first Christmas Eve almost the entire staff met up at The Parisian pub shortly after we closed at midday. I had asked Sue to join us as she was not working that morning. What I didn't realise was that it was traditional for "Santa snogs" to take place in the Parisian. The pub was on two levels and "mistletoe corner" was pitched discreetly in a quiet alcove at the bottom of the stairs. The boys waited eagerly for their turn, chatting with Sue and I and watching from our vantage point on the balcony. It took ages to complete the 'Santa Snog' although no-one seemed to mind. When it was all over Sue turned to me and said, "I have spoilt your fun haven't I?" I replied with a genuine "Not at all!". It had actually been great fun looking down on mistletoe corner and watching the various degrees of interest in the meeting of lips. They were all lovely girls but there were one or two I did not mind missing out on. Thanks to Sue!

THE SUBS WERE ON

The replacement reps soon arrived. There was Peter Collis from Derby, and David George from the Potteries. They were both popular additions. Although short in stature, Peter's footballing skills were a real benefit to our occasional matches against other regions and professional firms. David was a tall fair-haired lad from the potteries and remains a good friend to this day.

The reps seemed to be very close to the grapevine and aware of future moves before anyone else. David in particular appeared to be "in the know". We constantly nagged him to release the latest news. So much so that he became known as "spill the beans George". He did on occasions, but probably unfairly we always thought he was holding something back. Our suspicions may have been fuelled by his tendency to turn bright red when questioned

CLOSED ALL HOURS

During the summer of 1977 a strange request came from our Regional office. As the location of a branch was known to be vital to its success, the powers that be had decided to move the Leeds office in Hanley to larger premises in a much better location. The new site had previously been occupied by The Halifax who in turn were moving to even lager premises. The existing Leeds office had a requirement in the lease that meant the site had to be occupied until the lease was either reassigned or it expired. The solution was to place one of us in the old office during opening hours. We were instructed to keep the door open even though we were unable to carry out any business. Our job therefore was to tactfully explain the position and redirect customers to our new location about 400 yards away. Several of our team sat alone for a week at a time in the dim lighting slowly going mad. The transition went on for weeks as staff from across the region were assigned to share this thankless task.

KEEPING US AMUSED

The arrival of new trainees Andrew Finney and Guy Fenney made the office even more crowded. Andrew had dark hair and a matching moustache. He looked a bit like Charlie Chaplin but moved at such a slow pace we called him the "slow motion Charlie Chaplin".

Guy was an excellent sportsman with a special talent for both rugby and cricket. He proudly evidenced his involvement in a serious contact sport by regularly removing the plate supporting his false front teeth. Not a pretty sight. The increase in staff and consequent crowded workspace led to Andy and I, the old hands, trying to find reasons to get a breath of fresh air outside the branch whenever we could.

At this time, when mortgage applicants borrowed a high percentage we needed to take out a guarantee with the Royal Insurance thus protecting the Society if we were forced to repossess the property and sell at a loss. The Royal's offices were only a few yards away so Andy and I would personally take the applications round to the Royal for on the spot approval. There was one rather attractive assistant working there called Maxine that Andy was particularly keen on visiting. She became known to Andy as "the ravishing Maxine". These visits to the Royal were made as frequently as possible until Andy and the ravishing Maxine became an item, albeit briefly.

At Christmas time Andy and I paid the usual visit to nearby Lloyds bank to deposit cash and cheques before heading off to Rackhams department store just a couple of hundred yards in the opposite direction. We zoomed up the escalators to the top floor, which housed the toy department. It was expanded at Christmas time to fill the whole floor. Making no pretence to buy anything we headed straight for the scalextric racing cars and the Hornby railway to play. What fun to be big kids.

NO SUCH THING AS A FREE LUNCH?

After he had been there a few months I suggested to David "spill the beans" George we could meet up with some of my old work colleagues at Wragge & Co to see if we could do business. I was still playing football for Wylde Green with one of their solicitors, a guy called Roger Mason. I introduced David to Roger and was delighted to be invited by David to accompany them to the popular Waterloo Grill for a splendid lunch. My plan worked well as Roger was able to support us with some investment funds, and I gained valuable preparation for my future role as a rep.

With the branch being over staffed we weren't always too busy so started to incorporate silly games into our working day. One such game challenged trainees to avoid using commonly used words on the telephone such as 'branch' or 'cash'. This meant we all listened intently to every phone conversation, as the culprit would be fined a few coppers for each forbidden word uttered. At the end of the week in order to win the pot you had to introduce into the phone conversation a previously agreed unusual phrase. The one that stands out was "Have you seen the pigeons in the churchyard?". A standing ovation occurred one afternoon when Andy delivered the line whilst on the phone to, of all people, Spiny, the Regional Manager.

Much fun was had at our crowded section of the office. It was often hard to keep the noise down due to the ever-increasing number of trainees. There were so many I can't recall them all, but I do remember that one new recruit had a particular problem. During one cashiering training session with Joy it became obvious that she was not happy. She cut short the session to have a quiet word with Glynn concerning the trainee's personal hygiene. Knowing Joy's usual straightforward style we were surprised that she did not tackle the issue head on, but none of us were keen to have a word either. In the end a canister of Right Guard deodorant was placed in the new trainee's till. Poor chap he must have found the situation very difficult, but it seemed to solve the problem and was soon forgotten.

TO THE TOWER

Almost out of nowhere someone suggested we have a branch outing to Blackpool. To enable everyone, including partners to go it had to be either a Sunday or bank holiday. We chose the August bank holiday and guess what? It poured down! We were determined not to let that bother us, so undeterred along with our macs and our partners we boarded the coach outside the branch and set off for the M6. We had only driven a few miles along the motorway when the coach drifted to a halt. The driver got out and opened the engine cover to diagnose the problem. He was soon back on board asking if anyone had something similar to a fan belt to enable a temporary repair. After much head shaking and several inappropriate comments Andrew Finney (the slow-motion Charlie Chaplin) put his hand up. He volunteered the use of the cord from his anorak. The driver took it gratefully, made a miraculous mend, and we were back on the move.

Despite the poor weather it was an enjoyable day enabling our respective partners to get to know each other, and a good deal of staff bonding to take place. The driver managed to have a proper repair carried out while we were at play and we returned home safely, wet and tired, but happy.

CELEBRATIONS

The prolific turnover of staff was a real bonus for leaving do's. There seemed to be one virtually every week. As they were nearly all linked to promotion or other positive moves morale at these events was always high. Our favourite venue was The Parisian pub, a stone's throw from the branch. Although no one smoked the celebratory atmosphere sometimes led to the emergence of small cigars. These were usually Cafe Cremes displayed in a smart little tin, or occasionally the more expensive square shaped individually wrapped Villiger Export. We all joined in even though we knew it was a bit silly as we didn't inhale, it was merely an affectation.

Particularly memorable celebrations were held when David "spill the beans" George received his pink envelope confirming his promotion to branch manager at Sheldon; and when Peter Collins was moved onwards and upwards to another local branch at nearby Great Barr.

OUR TURN

All this upward movement became unsettling for the three amigos. Andy and I had been tracking the progress of trainees across the country. We built up a record of all the newly appointed reps including the date they joined and their appointment to area representative. This was made possible as all new appointments were confirmed and circulated between branches. Promotions were most rapid in the South East, particularly in London. This was mainly due to the even greater turnover of staff down there. It also didn't escape our notice that age was a factor with the older trainees moving more quickly.

Just as we started to think we were being overlooked Andy got the call from Regional Office. Given that nearly all the recent moves had been within the Midlands region, Andy was a little surprised that he was being sent many miles East to the Norwich branch. He was delighted to hear the news of his promotion, but naturally a little apprehensive. The cigars were lit and Andy was off in his brand new Mini 1000.

By this time the car policy had changed with reps now being allocated a Mini rather than the dated and somewhat unreliable Hillman Imp. Andy had only been gone a few weeks when I received the news that Wolverhampton branch would be my new home for my stint as an Area Rep. I was delighted as I could live at home and commute every day in my new bright (Java) green company Mini 1000. It also meant that I could now sell my Imp, which was beginning to play up even when the ignition key was dry!

The other big plus was that I could continue to see Sue on a regular basis, allowing our blossoming relationship to strengthen. We had just come back from a very enjoyable ten days in Majorca enjoying the sunshine and the sangria. An unexpected highlight of the trip was a conducted tour of the huge American aircraft carrier; 'John F Kennedy'. Our holiday rep had a high ranking "friend" on board who had offered to take a small group of tourists around the impressive vessel. It had a crew of 7000 with its own newspaper and TV station. It was amazing!

The further training at Temple Row had been very useful. I had experienced the workings of a large city centre branch and had even spent time training new recruits. Working with the reps was also excellent preparation for becoming one myself.

Life was good. Things were going really well with work and play, so with just one more leaving do to attend I set off for my next adventure.

CHAPTER 3
WOLVERHAMPTON
OCTOBER 1977 TO JULY 1979

THE TOWN

Situated approximately 20 miles to the north west of my home in Birmingham, the industrial city of Wolverhampton has a population of just over 250,000.

Industry grew rapidly in the 1800's due to substantial coal and iron deposits. The Mander family whose wealth was built from varnish and paint production dominated the area for many years.

For over 100 years it was a major manufacturer of bicycles. The last producer, Viking, had been in operation since 1868 and at its peak in 1965 produced over 20,000 bikes. The last bike was wheeled out in 1975.

It became a City as part of the millennium celebrations in 2000. It has the 2nd highest percentage of Sikhs at just over 9% due to an influx from the Punjab between 1935 and 1973.

The city has successfully attracted new investment and recently secured commitment from Jaguar Land Rover. Their new factory built over 300,000 engines in 2017 becoming the busiest engine factory in the UK.

DAY ONE

I had picked up my sparkling new Mini 1000 from Cox & Co in Regent Street Leeds the week before I was due to start as the Area Representative at the Leeds branch in Wolverhampton.

I didn't go straight there on my first day as the Regional Manager, Norman Weatherhead (AKA Spiny) had asked me to call in to see him on the way. Spiny was his usual positive and motivational self. He gave me a real pep talk and presented me with a copy of Dale Carnegie's book "How to Win Friends and Influence People" and stressed that it was essential reading. He finished our chat with these words; "always be yourself, and therefore to thine own self be true". The second half of this advice is a quote from Hamlet's Polonius. Amusingly the same character is also known for "neither a borrower or a lender be". By working for a building society I was striving to become both!

After leaving Erdington with Spiny's motivational words bouncing around my head and Carnegie's book safely tucked away in my brand new Leeds leather briefcase, I joined the M6 at the nearby Spaghetti Junction. I had only driven through the famous multi-layered junction on a couple of occasions and made sure I followed the correct signs. The stretch to the Wolverhampton turn off was one of the busiest in the country and when I later experienced it at rush hour I decided to call it "death race 2000" after the film of the same name that came out a couple of years earlier (1975). It had occasional vehicle holdups, which forced me to take a much slower journey along the Birmingham New Road.

ARRIVING AT THE BRANCH

The layout of the branch was unique. It had two separate counters. The ground floor had four till positions and opened out onto Victoria Street directly opposite Beatties, the department store. From the banking hall there were steps up to the second counter area where three till positions could be found with the entrance opening out into the covered Mander centre. The steps were open but carpeted to match the two banking areas. It became my "party piece" to firmly lock my feet into a gap and lean forward facing up the stairs to imitate a ski Jumper. Eddie the Eagle Duffin took off.

My new manager was Malcolm Bason. In his late forties, he was one of the older managers. He was slightly above average height with fair hair and glasses that struggled to contain the very thick lenses correcting severe short sightedness. Malcolm had three grown up children and was married to Pam who ran an office cleaning business, whose clients included our branch.

He sat me down in his office and told me what he expected of me. He had been at the branch for a number of years and given his age was unlikely to progress further. He went on to outline his expectations. Given my young age (just 24) he wanted me to concentrate on the younger end of the professional community, as he knew many of the older generation. I could see the logic in this approach but was then in for a shock. Less than two hours on from the meeting with my Regional Manager who had told me to be myself, Malcolm was now insisting that I should be "all things to all men"! I would choose the former.

His second plan was for me to be responsible for the full collecting agents. Owned by firms such as estate agents and solicitors they acted like mini branches but with limited facilities such as deposits and restricted withdrawals.

The branch covered a huge area right across to the Welsh coast. The main agencies could be found in Shifnal, Penkridge, Newport (Shropshire), Bilston, Bridgnorth, Wellington and Cannock. By far and away the largest was Cannock. Boot and Son was a well-established firm of estate agents and property valuers. There were two Boots (father and son) both called Tim. It was such a successful Leeds agent that it took in more money than some of the smallest Leeds branches. In addition to young and old Tim there was George Scotney who carried out most of the property valuations.

The role of looking after the agents included stationery and advertising deliveries and sorting out any problems. It would involve a considerable amount of travelling. This appealed to me as the proud owner of my new Mini 1000.

THE SET UP

It's a small world and could be described as cramped when you find you are too close to someone you find it difficult to get on with. I knew that the previous rep was none other than BBB who I had the somewhat dubious pleasure of spending a couple of days with at Acocks Green. I thought he had already gone but he had been asked to spend a day with me before he moved on to manage his first branch.It was a complete waste of my time and his. There was some sort of call record that he skipped over mainly because it appeared to contain very little. He found it difficult to tell me who his best professional introducers were. The reason would soon become clear. He quickly disappeared and I knew straight away that I would pretty much be on my own.

Things looked up when I met the chief clerk Terry Matthews. Mid-twenties with a friendly smile and very keen to help, he was a good chap to know. He didn't try to change my view of BBB and confirmed that I would be lucky to find many contacts that knew him. Terry couldn't be more supportive and we worked well together and I could see he had potential to progress to management.

Unfortunately, the same couldn't be said of the three management trainees; Mike, Dave and Graham. They were all nice lads and also very keen to help but they seemed to lack the drive and energy to progress further. The need for a strategically placed boot came to mind. Mike was a keen cricketer with an unusual dress sense or perhaps lack of one. Dave was quiet and completely under the thumb of his girlfriend who was around so often I initially thought she was part of the staff.

Last but not least was Graham. I liked Graham. Short with a slightly rounded physique and aged 25 going on 45, he was so old fashioned that he still referred to the street as the "hos rad" (translated from black country - horse road). He talked about the old days as if they were still about.

There were five girls. Christine and Ann R had been there a while and had earned more responsibility. They were both really helpful and efficient. Christine was quite classy in terms of both approach and appearance. I was told that Christine had previously been the Regional Manager's PA and it showed. Ann R (there were two Ann's) was more down to earth and shared Mike's dress sense. She was also very efficient and dedicated.

The other Ann was Ann Marie. She was attractive with large eyes, and not short of confidence. She had Malcolm wrapped around her little finger. She was great with the customers and used her charm effectively. However Malcolm did prove he was boss when one Saturday morning in mid-summer Ann M turned up for work and it was obvious that a certain part of her attire had been left at home. Malcolm took her into his office and we were convinced Ann would be sent straight home to change. Out she came smiling and bounced up the stairs and took her place at the counter. To be fair to Malcolm it never happened again and normal dress was back on.

Dawn was a quiet girl who just got on with her work effectively. It was rumoured that her Dad knew Malcolm but she soon proved that she deserved he place in the team.

Last but not least was Julie. Fairly quiet but a loyal and reliable member of the team. If you had to put two people together as man and wife it would be Julie and Graham. It was therefore no surprise when they later became an item, followed by marriage. A good match and even better when the bride was driven along the "Hos Rad" to church in a vintage car.

OUT AND ABOUT

Malcolm was very much into a daily routine. He left the office at 11am and crossed the road to Beatties and made his way to where coffee was served. He would be joined by a small number of business contacts that were by this time also his friends. He took me across during the first week but I never returned, as these were clearly his generation and his contacts.

After returning to the office to make sure all was well and inspect the counter sheets to spot any large investments he would inform Terry, the Chief Clerk, that he was out for lunch and would return later. His regular lunchtime retreat was the Beckminster Club (AKA the Beck) just a short ride in Malcolm's Hillman Hunter. The car policy allocated the Hunter to those who had served 10 years as a branch manager. It was slightly larger than the standard Hillman Avenger but just as unremarkable.

The Beck was for members only but frequented by a wide range of ages. I was therefore encouraged to join. The steward was very "old school" referring to most people by their surnames. It took him a while to accept that I did not approve and he eventually dropped "Mr Duffin" and I became "sir" which was even more annoying. The Beck had a limited but very good menu and had the benefit of a snooker table that was wasted on me. I maintain that my inability with a snooker cue is the sign of a well-spent youth.

ONE FOR THE ROAD

Very quickly Malcolm wanted me to be formally introduced to his two favourite agents; Boot and Son (Cannock) and Pitt and Cooksey solicitors (Bridgnorth).

First stop was lunch with the Boots in Cannock Staffordshire. Both Tims were sizeable chaps and could easily match Malcolm for alcoholic consumption and that was saying something. We went to the Hollies one of the very few decent places for lunch.

Both of the Tim's were very down to earth and old Tim was forced by his son to tell us about his time in the war as a tank commander. He still looked like one. I looked at him and mentally placed a helmet on his head envisioning him peering menacingly out of his tank. Young Tim was keen to move the firm into the modern era. I thought this might be a challenge as dad was clearly still in charge and not keen to change too much. As I climbed back into the trusty Hillman Hunter, I began to recount the number of drinks that Malcolm had put away. The total made me think of opening the door and heading for the bus stop but I merely reached for the seat belt and plugged myself in and hoped for the best. Despite the alcohol and poor vision we made it back safely.

Next stop was Bridgnorth in Shropshire on the opposite side of Wolverhampton to Cannock. Situated in the Severn valley the attractive town is split into high town and low town.

Michael Cooksey (MC) ran the firm with no sign of a Mr Pitt. He was assisted by a young solicitor, Steve Whiston, who had qualified the year before (1977). This was similar to the Boots lunch with the young gun looking to change the world but meeting resistance from the senior man in charge. I felt comfortable with Steve but as far as MC was concerned many words spring to mind so I will stop at "not my cup of tea". A strange looking man in his late forties, he had an upper set of teeth that were rather further forward than nature intended.

Before leaving the office I had been warned by both Terry and Ann R that P&C lunches were boozy affairs and every single rep had suffered from the "induction ceremony". I very carefully counted my intake and tried to keep a watchful eye on the old boys, but I failed miserably. I managed to consume the beautifully presented desert but almost immediately I was in a mad dash for the loo. I will spare the details but the extra money paid over to the restaurant will provide a clue as to the extent of my suffering. I don't know with what or how they ambushed me but I was well and truly scuppered.

My day continued to fall apart. I had left my Mini on Malcolm's drive. He did not take any blame and insisted I take refuge in his house and drink plenty of water and try to recover. As soon as we pulled up on his drive in front of a very smart modern detached house the nausea returned so fast I only manage to get my head out of the car before repeating the earlier release.

I was horrified to see Malcolm's wife Pam was at home as she ran up the drive. However she was immediately on my side and was giving Malcolm what for. I suspect she had seen it all before. It was now obvious that I was in no fit state to drive home and I bunkered down at chez Bason's for the night. My hangover was made worse by the constant "I told you so" that I heard repeatedly throughout the following day.

PROPERTY LADDER

Malcolm did not mention the disastrous Bridgnorth lunch again. However I asked if MC was serious when he brought up the possibility of selling the ground floor of his High Street premises to the Leeds to create a new branch office. Malcolm said it was something he would talk to Norman (Spiny) about.

In the meantime he told me I should be looking to buy a property in Wolverhampton. I sensed that Spiny was involved and decided to start looking without any real intention of actually buying somewhere. There were several reasons for holding back. Firstly I couldn't afford to buy anywhere half decent even with a subsidised mortgage. Secondly Sue and I were certainly "going steady" but commitment had not been discussed. Finally by the time I had found somewhere I would be close to being made a branch manager, who knows where!

Despite my mate Andy being far away in deepest East Anglia we still managed to meet up occasionally. His girlfriend Sue was still living and working in Birmingham
and he came home to see her quite often. In the summer the four of us drove down in our Minis to Newquay in Cornwall for a week's holiday in a B&B. I can't say it was a great success. My Sue and I got on really well but Andy and his Sue didn't get on quite so well. The B&B was like a down market version of Fawlty Towers with the owner questioning as to who had left their peas. By the time the holiday was over the Sue and Andy relationship was too.

Andy had rented a flat a few miles outside Norwich and added a few basic pieces of furniture including my mum's old drop leaf dining table. Renting a flat was an expense I was very grateful to avoid. As he was on his own he had the company of Eric the dog for a few months until Andy decided it was unfair on Eric to be out of the flat all day and found a good home of full time dog lovers who welcomed Eric.

The lovely Terri who was a rep for the City of London building society replaced Eric. It was a whirlwind romance with the wedding set for September '79 just nine months after they met and with me delighted to be asked to be best man!

THE MARKET

The British economy was still in a vulnerable state and interest rates soared. The mortgage rate hit a high of 15%. The only good news was that savers were also receiving higher rates. The Leeds had resisted introducing Term Share accounts for good logical reasons but now serious competition forced their introduction. We called ours "High Return Shares" and launched them with advertisements featuring jet planes (albeit plastic ones) zooming to new heights. They took off immediately.

Business was good at the Leeds and new branches were still being opened across the country. I had started to make some useful business contacts particularly one young solicitor whose father was a senior partner and known to Malcolm. Somewhat surprisingly Malcolm's strategy was beginning to pay dividends.

The clearing banks were starting to compete particularly in the mortgage market. My first few bank visits were a bit strange as there was little evidence of calls from previous reps as banks were still a reasonable source of savings funds. When I asked to see the securities clerk, I was often greeted by the sight of an old green Leeds investment folder containing literature from some time ago. The dust was blown off but I was keen to swap it for a new blue folder. To be fair the area was so huge that it was impossible to cover every contact.

Up at HO in Leeds the Chief General Manager Leonard Hyde stood down and became President. Stanley Walker replaced him and a fresh impetus was expected.

THE RIGHT COURSE

Having been very fortunate to be supported with day release at Birmingham and secure three of the required six subjects required to become an associate of the Chartered Institute I was keen to carry on. Unfortunately there was no college support available locally and I thought hard about how to progress. I had one compulsory subject left which was "Financial accounting and control". It was the hardest subject evidenced by the pass rate being significantly below all the other subjects. I decided to leave that one until last. I chose Personnel Management and Building Society Law and Practice as the next two to attempt.

With no local college available I had to make a decision, should I go down the correspondence course route or do my own thing? I was completely turned off by the former, as there seemed to be a considerable amount of time spent on areas unlikely to turn up in the exam. I decided the self-tuition route was the best way forward. This could be supported by the excellent revision courses run by the Institute at Fanhams Hall. My mate Andy was in a similar position and decided to do the same.

It was a gamble but I went ahead and bought the recommended books and past exam papers and got to work. It was a help that I found both subjects very interesting particularly personnel management. The revision courses at Fanhams Hall were hard work but extremely beneficial. Andy and I also enjoyed a few pints at the bar. When the results came both Andy I were overjoyed when we found out we had passed them both. Five down, lust one to go.
HIP HOP

I loved playing football at the weekends and had suffered a few injuries over the years but nothing serious. That all changed at the end of my first year at Wolverhampton in October 1978. Wylde Green C.O.B were my regular Saturday afternoon team. I picked up and injury and missed a couple of games. I was also playing for a Sunday morning team from the New Inn pub at the Swan, Yardley.

When I thought I was fit to return to action I opted to start on a Sunday. I was playing up front and the game was in full swing when I was put clean through with only the keeper to beat. I did just that but as the ball was heading for goal the keeper came through and took my right leg out. I screamed as my leg was removed from the hip joint.

A crowd quickly gathered and I begged those able to look to hold my leg above the ground at the least painful angle. It was obviously a serious injury made worse by the fact that there was an ambulance strike. The good news was that the match was being played at one of the car factories that had its own ambulance. I was swiftly taken to East Birmingham hospital (now named Heartlands) where I was given a high dose of Valium and my dislocated hip was rotated back into place.

When my senses returned my right leg was hanging in the air with wide strips of Elastoplast down each side. I was in both traction and shock. On arrival at the orthopedic ward I was informed that I would be "strung up" for four to five weeks and probably off work for four months.

I was only in the ward for a few minutes when I heard a group chanting as they approached. It was my team mates who were swiftly ejected with only the manager allowed to remain. I told him the prognosis with the addition that I would be unlikely to play competitive football again. He said there was good news as I was covered by insurance for a relatively modest amount whilst off work. My Mum and Sue were the next to arrive with my poor Mum struggling to hold back the "I told you not to play so often". Sue was very sympathetic and they both promised to visit regularly, which they did.

There were four of us with our legs in the air at the far end of the long open ward. In the two beds opposite were Rob, a policeman in his early twenties and a stroppy biker called Dave. Rob had driven into the back of a stationary car when blinded by the low sun. Dave the biker wouldn't give precise details but we suspected he had just fallen off. Big Ron was in the next bed to me. He had gone through the windscreen of his friend's car and was lucky to have only broken his leg and suffered cuts and bruises. Ron was a young butcher whose favourite word was "stoat".

All four of us were in traction but mine was very different. The others had all suffered broken femurs and needed to be in traction for a much longer time this meant a bolt had to be inserted through the leg to enable long term hanging. It also meant that they all had to have a regular Heparin injection to prevent blood clots.

The rock singer Ian Dury had just released his bestselling single. As the nurse approached with syringe in hand we would burst into "hit me with that Heparin stick, Hit me, Hit me,"

The nurses were good fun and game for a laugh. We were not ill, just trapped and this forced us to look for any entertainment however daft. My Mum (Olive) was a star. I persuaded her to bring some beers in for the boys and she duly obliged. She was about five feet two very slim and wouldn't say boo to a goose. On the day of our beer delivery I had been explaining to the boys and some of the nurses that Olive had been one of the very few women tank drivers in the Second World War but didn't like to talk about it. There wasn't a grain of truth in this but amazingly they all swallowed my yarn. As Olive waddled down the ward carefully balancing the tins of beer the looks of astonishment people's faces were a picture. Before anyone had chance to question my Mum, I told her why she had become the focus of attention. My apologies were soon accepted as she could take a joke. Dear old Mum, bless her.

Malcolm was great and even managed to bring over my favourite starter from the Beckminster; egg mayonnaise together with a decanter full of port. I am not sure if this was my favourite but the port made me popular as I shared it on the ward.

The initial time schedule turned out to be very accurate as I missed over four months of work, as I could not drive until all support was removed and I could fully weight bear.

My contract stipulated that my salary decreased as the time off grew. Malcolm and Spiny appealed for full pay on my behalf. I was told that the issue was taken to the new Chief General Manager Stanley Walker who thankfully pronounced in my favour. I received full pay plus football insurance and had no way of spending it. My savings swelled.

Not long before my enforced absence my car had been changed. The slightly larger Talbot Sunbeam replaced the Mini. Talbot was the new name for Hillman but the Leeds increasingly strange car policy did not cover the extra cost of a rear parcel shelf. I was happy for my car to be kept back at the branch for others to use mainly the Chief Clerk, Terry.

FOLLOWING THE LEEDER

News came down from HO that a new monthly in-house paper was to be launched. Since 1946 there had been a company magazine called "the Permanent Light". The Light came out each quarter and focused away from mainstream business with sections such as gardening notes and competitions. I particularly enjoyed the caption competition where you had to add a caption to a cartoon. I won it on several occasions but was not sure if there were many other entries. The new paper would sit alongside "the Light" focusing on business and staff news.

All staff were invited to put forward a name for the new venture. After much thought I decided to enter the name: "High Society". Not surprisingly it didn't win, in fact Malcolm said it sounded more like something you would find on the top shelf in a newsagents. I had not realised he had an interest in that area.

As the first edition came out of the Envopak in November 78 we discovered that the winning name was "The Leeder". It was a much more appropriate title. It was very popular with a good balance between business and pleasure. All staff appointments were featured enabling you to follow the progress of friends and acquaintances.

BRANCHING OUT

When I eventually returned to work Malcolm couldn't wait to tell me the latest news. Head Office had agreed the purchase with Pitt and Cooksey for the ground floor of their High Street premises in Bridgnorth. Not just that but Spiny told him that I was being 'penciled in' as manager.

My initial reaction was very positive but I then thought of having to see MC every day. I decided to look on the bright side. Malcolm suggested that I should start to look at houses in the area. A discussion with Sue turned into a fairly unromantic but practical proposal of marriage that thankfully Sue accepted. I then did what all good future son-in-laws did and approached Sue's dad (Tom) for his approval. I think he was pleased but was slightly put off balance when he said; "if you're sure". I was.

The premises were already used as offices and it was said that planning permission was all but guaranteed with the planning meeting set for a couple of weeks' time. Sue and I found a nice semi detached house on the Well Meadow estate close to the river. Probably too close.

MC was extremely confident that planning was "nailed on". But it wasn't. Not only did we lose but also the technicalities meant that it would be months before it would be passed, if ever. All bets were off. Well not quite all. We pulled out of the house purchase but continued to plan the wedding set for October.

GIVE IT A GO

To take my mind off the Bridgnorth non-event I decided to have a go at the remaining subject I needed to qualify. I had no knowledge of accounts but still took the somewhat brave or reckless decision to attempt the financial accounting and control paper without any formal tuition. I bought the recommended book by I think Williams and secured the past papers. I was really pinning my hopes on the refresher course at Fanhams Hall. I turned up for the course with Andy but with very little, if any, knowledge. I sat on the front row hoping this would help the flow of knowledge to my brain. It didn't.

For two whole days I tried to make sense of the lecturer's presentations. As I was sat right in front of him he asked me on more than one occasion to answer on of his questions. I failed every time. Near the end of the course he turned to me again and said, "here is your chance to get one right as it is a fifty-fifty question". I got it wrong.

What I did get was a stack of crib sheets to memorise. I decided to learn several key areas off by heart. One of them was the source and application of funds statement. At the end of May 1979, I arrived at the exam centre a little nervous but keen to have a go. I turned the paper over and was delighted to see a compulsory question on the source and application of funds carrying 25 marks. Having memorised the crib sheet I knew exactly how to complete it and was confident on obtaining most, if not all, of the marks. This only left about another 25 marks from the reaming four questions. When the results sheet arrived I read it several times just to make sure it said PASS. I was also delighted to see that the pass rate was the lowest of all the subjects at 31%. I was now an Associate of the Chartered Building Society Institute and could put the letters ACBSI after my name. There was also a cash reward from the Society and later an invitation to an awards lunch at HO.

A BRIDGE TOO FAR

A couple of months after the aborted move to Bridgnorth I received the call advising me of my new appointment. Bridgwater in Somerset replaced Bridgnorth. I knew where it was having experienced the traffic jams that regularly occurred before the M5 was extended. I was a little disappointed that it was so far from home but also intrigued that I had been given an existing branch as most reps were going to new branches.

It was all happening at once. New job, new home to find and a wedding to organise. I said goodbye to the team at Wolverhampton with my leaving gift tucked underneath my arm. Fashion dictated that my hair was still slightly on the long side but my new hairdryer would keep it in shape.

I would be leaving Sue at home to plan the wedding whilst I searched for a home and settled in to management.

I had learnt how to develop new business and trust my instincts when assessing people. I was also qualified and felt ready to run my own branch. Great change was afoot with the addition of leaving home and getting married. Exciting times beckoned.

CHAPTER 4
BRIDGWATER
JULY 1979 TO MAY 1981

THE TOWN

With a population of just over 40,000 Bridgwater sits astride
the River Parrett on the edge of the Somerset Levels.
Originally a thriving port and trading centre, it is mentioned in
both the Domesday Book and the earlier Anglo-Saxon
Chronicle dating from around 800 A.D.
Today Bridgwater is an important industrial centre producing
plastics, engine parts, chemicals and foods. Being close to the
M5, it also boasts two major distribution centres.

WHY WAS I THERE?

The branch had been open for a while and I was its third
manager. I was keen to discover what was going on down
there. I booked into the Royal Clarence Hotel as instructed by
the South West Regional Manager's PA. The journey down
the M5 on the Sunday afternoon was straightforward. The
Clarence turned out to be only a few yards from the branch on
the High Street close to The Cornhill.

After checking in at the comfortable, yet somewhat dated,
hotel I strolled over to my new branch. The good news was
that it was located in the heart of the town opposite the
Cornhill next door to a small M&S store. The bad news was
that it was slightly set back from the road on a bend and was
therefore easily missed if you didn't know what you were
looking for. Two columns on either side of the entrance
ensured that it was almost invisible! It did boast two very nice
plant troughs on either side of the central doorway but with the
columns, the bend and the set back from the pavement, they
didn't really help.

DAY ONE

That first morning I waited patiently for the branch to be opened before I put in an appearance. I was immediately struck by the size of the banking hall, and almost (literally) struck by an equally enormous cheese plant. It was huge and I felt like David Bellamy as I foraged through its extensive foliage towards the standard Leeds polished wooden counter, where Mike Bowen the Chief Clerk met me.

Mike and I had met previously on the new trainees' induction course four years ago back in 1975. Mike was about 40 with short dark hair and of trim build. He was a Somerset boy and retained the local burr. Mike was married to Margaret, and they both had two children from their first marriages. He told me that the current, yet soon to depart, manager Jim Browning would be able to meet me later. There was something in the way Mike advised me of Jim's late arrival that made me think that this would not be a straightforward handover, which was set to last two weeks.

Mike introduced me to the two girls. Carol had apparently experienced a tough year but had just found out she was pregnant. With short dark hair and a southeast accent she seemed the picture of health. Her southeast accent was in stark contrast to Julie's local twang. She was tall with shoulder length dark hair. Carol was married to Rob, a social worker and Julie's husband Nick was, I think, in the building trade. All three gave me a warm welcome.

Jim strolled in mid-morning. He looked like a young Harry Secombe with wavy dark hair and a full figure on a short frame. All I had been told in advance was that Jim was due to leave the Leeds in a couple of weeks. He wasn't exactly friendly. He stood in the doorway, announced that he would see me tomorrow, and exited hastily.

Mike seemed to have more time for me starting with a tour of my new domain. The branch had previously been a bank with a full size walk-in safe that would have swallowed more than twenty of our tiny safes. This vast space was now used for storage. There was the usual kitchen area and a table for staff but the Manager's office was more like the 'Black Hole of Calcutta'. It was tiny and had no natural light although it did have a curtain along the wall behind the desk in order to give the impression that with one swift swish a large window and bright sunlight would be revealed. It wasn't! The whole room smelt of damp. My initial thought, which proved to be correct, was that if ever there was an incentive to get out and develop business, this was it.

BECOMING CLEARER

Mike and I sat down in 'the black hole' as my office became affectionately known, with a cup of tea as I tried to get a better picture of the situation. We started on business performance. Mike offered several good reasons for the relatively low level of business for an established branch. Firstly, there was strong competition with the top three UK building societies being located on the same street, plus the very strong local Bridgwater Building Society just across the road. The second problem was the branch's almost invisible frontage. Thirdly, Mike pointed out our obvious geographical remoteness from our Yorkshire base, with the nearest Leeds branch being over 40 miles away. He recalled how slow business was when the branch opened in 1974. One Saturday morning had passed without a single customer. To be fair the launch wasn't helped by an advertisement in the Bridgwater Mercury designed to promote the opening, giving the address as 8, Cross Cheaping, COVENTRY. They were all fair points and were unfortunately difficult to argue with.

We moved on to the turnover of managers. Mike explained that the first manager, David Honey, was someone he respected but who had limited branch experience as he had only worked at HO prior to his appointment. David soon discovered that managing a branch was not for him and opted to return to Yorkshire via a spell at Plymouth branch. Mike was politely non-committal about the absent Jim, which said a lot in itself. He had come from the much larger branch in Bristol without any prior warning or explanation. He was described as both a people person and law unto himself. Not having had the chance to get to know him I couldn't possibly comment. Mike pointed out that Jim had increased the business, particularly in mortgages, although not always to the satisfaction of the Regional Manager. I was beginning to hope the handover would not last the scheduled fortnight.

A LONG TWO WEEKS.

The next day Jim took me to meet a couple of our associates who carried out house valuations for mortgage purposes. At Greenslades I met valuer Charles Scott, a well-spoken, friendly chap. He was also an astute businessman, not missing the opportunity to pass me some brochures for houses that were selling in the area which he thought might be of interest to me. He recommended a modern three-bed semi in the nearby village of Cannington. I promised to have a peep.

The next visit was to a pub where Jim was clearly no stranger. He was a gregarious character who seemed to know a lot of the local professional people, including Trish, a lively lady who ran a recruitment agency. Jim introduced us and, emulating Charles' business style, I took the opportunity to mention that Sue was an excellent shorthand typist and trained cashier. Trish promised to see what she could do when Sue moved down to Bridgwater in a few weeks' time.

I took the opportunity to ask Jim why he was leaving. He didn't really answer the question but told me he was seeking 'a new challenge' and had 'a few irons in the fire'. I never did find out what that meant.

NIGHT AT THE ROUND TABLE

The following day Jim called me in to his office and insisted that I accompany him to an evening event where I would meet some useful contacts. I had never been to a Round Table meeting before, but I knew it's aim was to develop business interests, serve the community and was targeted at professionals under the age of 40. I was, to say the least, sceptical.

This particular event was a dinner where the drinks flowed faster than the River Parrett. To my horror and potential embarrassment, the after-dinner entertainment was joke telling. Taking turns around the room each guest was tasked with delivering a funny. I have never been able to remember jokes let alone tell one in public. Realising there was no escape my first thought was where I was placed in the batting order. I took some comfort to see I was somewhere in the middle. I began to rack my brain.

I was rather relieved that the standard of the first couple of jokes was pretty poor. All I needed was any old joke. Anything! I looked at the menu for inspiration. "Oh no, not that one!" I thought to myself, but nothing else sprang to mind. As I stood up I shakily began the tale of the whale that gave a poorly squid a lift to the surface of the water. As he bumped into his old friend the shark, the whale off loaded the squid saying, "Hi Fred, here's that six quid (sick squid) I owe you". The old ones are the best! Not a great joke but it got me off the hook, so to speak.

As the Round Tablers became more desperate to entertain, the standard sank even lower and the noise increased. It was a very boozy affair attended by very few potential contacts. I vowed never to join despite later encouragement from my boss.

ONE SECRET AGENT

Having now met most of the local contacts Jim and I set off to visit the full collecting agencies which acted as mini branches. The two main ones were at Street and Wellington. Street is a large village which lies about 14 miles to the east of Bridgwater and just a couple of miles from Glastonbury. Home of Clarks, the shoe people, for more than 200 years, it still has its head office there. Our local agents, Resfair, did reasonably well but business was still fairly modest in comparison with my experience of agencies back in the Midlands.

Taylors, the Wellington based estate agents had a far more substantial inflow of business. The town was about 14 miles to the south west of Bridgwater and 7 miles to the west of the county town of Taunton. Larger than Street, with a population of around 14,000 it relied heavily on Relyon beds and aerosol manufacturing. I couldn't put my finger on it but was a little unsure of the one-man band.

By far the strangest agency that we visited was at Castle Cary. Just over 25 miles to the east of Bridgwater the small town with deserted streets seemed an unlikely home for business. The owner was listed as an insurance broker, but rather confusingly Jim shepherded me into a pet shop. Jim was reluctant to explain how the appointment had been made, but I felt sure we were barking up the wrong tree!

What became clear to me was that the absence of full branch representation was a real limitation to business development in Somerset. It seemed a major omission not to have a branch in the county town of Taunton whose population was more than Bridgwater, Street and Wellington put together. I also realised that we had probably missed the boat as all our main competitors were already firmly established in Taunton. I was to be consistently reminded of this by reluctant introducers in the coming weeks.

ALONE AT LAST

After a long two weeks I was glad to wave Jim on his way and be on my own and start to get a grip of my new situation. My Regional Manager was a friendly guy called Mike Rooke. He telephoned me from his office in Bristol, both to welcome me and ask me for a favour. My new boss Mike was in his forties, of slim build with little hair and gold-rimmed glasses. He explained that following his departure Jim's car would need to be returned to HO, and due to our remoteness, I was tasked with driving it back to Leeds. I was not particularly happy, having already spotted it in the car park with (inexplicably) several large lumps of concrete stuck to the sills, but duly obliged.

Jim's car, being a Ford Cortina, indicated that he had been a manager for at least ten years. It was well used and looked as though it had never been cleaned since the day he collected it in place of his Hillman Hunter.

The increasingly strange Leeds' car policy had recently reached a new low. The Ford Cortina had replaced the aging Hillman Hunter but came without a radio as standard. However, less experienced managers who weren't eligible for a Cortina were supplied with a new model Talbot Horizon which came complete with radio. This lack of radio parity led to a bizarre decision: the Society decided to PAY for the radio to be removed from each Talbot Horizon ensuring silent equality.

A previous and equally strange car policy decision not to pay for the parcel shelf in company Talbot Sunbeams led to a heated dispute when my friend and colleague Andy's Sunbeam was broken into on my stag night in Birmingham. His camera was stolen from the exposed boot and the insurance company refused his claim on the grounds that he had left it in an uncovered area. Quite rightly Andy fought his corner and eventually the Society coughed up compensation.

WEST SIDE STORY

Out of work time I was actively looking for a house for Sue and I to set up home. Virtually everyone told me to look on the west side of town. The main reason being that the British Cellophane factory was situated on the east side of town. Apart from producing huge amounts of cellophane, it emitted a pungent odour. As the prevailing wind blows from west to east it was advisable to live on the fresher west side.

I narrowed down my search to a number of suitably situated villages including Nether Stowey, North Petherton and

Cannington. I still had the Greenslades brochure for the semi in Cannington, a pretty village only three miles from the town centre. The recently decorated Wimpey house on Conway Road fitted the bill. Sue came down to view it, the price was affordable, and so we took the plunge. There were no carpets and we had no furniture but that didn't bother us. We knew it would be fun to put it all together.

Over the summer we worked hard on the house, with Sue coming down as often as she could. We got married back in our home town of Birmingham in the October, and happily began to feather our new nest. When we first moved in we had a portable black and white TV, a bed and a wardrobe that I had bought from my friend Paul Wells. We also had a rug that Sue and I put together (Readicut) covering much of the bare floor. We sat on deck chairs in front of the Rayburn boiler and admired its ability to heat water and a couple of radiators. The attached semi was a holiday home for a London based policeman who was very friendly but rarely visited. The rear garden backed on to a small caravan park that was home to mainly retired couples. We were in the country and we loved it. Ok so our small estate was located just off the road leading to the Hinkley Point nuclear power station, but what did we care? We couldn't actually see it and reasoned that if the plant went up so would most of Somerset.

THE BEARDED WONDER

Things were going well at the branch and I was delighted when my Regional Manager Mike Rooke rang to inform me that he was bringing the General Manager, Ted Germaine, to visit the branch. When the day came we were all on our best behaviour. Perhaps there was one exception as Mike the Chief Clerk had grown a beard. The ban on beards was not exactly a written rule, merely recognised as a defintite "No, no!". Mike was fully aware of the unofficial policy and I was happy to support him. The visit went well and Ted was his usual positive and cheerful self. The only surprise was when Mike Rooke told Ted that Mike had grown his beard for a part in a play, a completely erroneous 'fact' which Ted readily accepted. There was some truth in this as Mike was a keen am dram participant, but we all knew that the beard growing was not for any current role. The next day Mike Rooke rang and asked me to have a quiet word with Mike. I told him I already had and although I was aware of the unofficial policy I saw no harm. Mike was always smartly dressed and had excellent rapport with all our customers.

A few months later a regional management meeting was held in Bristol. Ted took the opportunity to attend and to also pop in to several local branches, including ours. As he left the building I overheard him muttering "bloody long run that play is having".

A few weeks later Mike and his wife Margaret decided to carry out some home improvements. Naturally they wanted to add this to their mortgage and take advantage of the staff rate. Their application progressed smoothly until the Regional Manager intervened. It transpired that mortgage approval was to be contingent on Mike removing the offending growth. Mike took it well adopting a bit of a "hair today, gone tomorrow attitude".

The earlier regional meeting in Bristol turned out to be an opportunity for learning new lessons. The South West region was a combination of English and Welsh branches but as I entered the room it was clear that this was not necessarily a friendly alliance. The large board table running the length of the room seemed to represent the divide of two nations with the Welsh on one side and the English on the other. The tension, or maybe it was playful banter, was palpable.

The room thawed a little when Ted entered the room and, after a general business update, he asked if there were any questions. Ted had mentioned earlier the possibility that the Leeds would consider a merger with another society as long as it proved to be a good fit. One of the managers from the south coast piped up, asking Ted: "should we start to talk to local societies and get the ball rolling|?" Ted found it hard not to laugh, but the rest of us didn't.

Mike Rooke then covered regional business and ended his session with a request for the sharing of any good business ideas. The same chap who had offered to begin merger negotiations described a recent initiative to improve awareness in his town. He explained how his team had filled their main window area with 100 inflated balloons displaying the legend: "Say the Leeds and you're smiling". Customers were invited to enter a competition to guess the total number of balloons displayed. When asked about the success of the promotion he said it had gone well until the heat from the spotlights caused the balloons to pop.

He described a desperate battle to keep the numbers at a steady 100. We were in fits of laughter. Ten out of ten for effort but I don't think many branches adopted the idea. It wasn't just the economy that was suffering the effects of inflation (I know, but I couldn't resist it).

However, one manager's idea was a galloping success. Howard Searle, the manager of the Exeter branch had dressed up in cowboy gear and called himself the "Loan Arranger". The national press got hold of the story and even the Daily Telegraph gave it prominence. It was Howard's 15 minutes of fame and it was well deserved.

SPOT THE JOB

After moving into our new house in Cannington it took a while for Sue to settle in to her new life. The main problem was Sue had to leave the Leeds as there were no other Leeds branches within commuting distance. I had heard nothing from Jim's friend Trish who ran the "Job Spot" recruitment agency. In November I bumped into her in town but when I reminded her about a possible position for Sue she looked a bit sheepish and explained that she didn't think I was serious. I am not sure why she took that view but was pleased to hear that she had lots of work and asked if Sue could call in to see her as soon as possible.

Sue was very quickly back at work and back to her usual self.

Trish started off placing Sue as a temp with the council as a "clerk plotter" in the planning department. They soon found out that Sue was a shorthanded typist and tried to persuade her to join full time, but life at the council was not for Sue. This was followed by a pleasant stint with local solicitors, Ash Clifford & Co. Then a real breakthrough came after Christmas when, after a successful temping job, Sue was offered a permanent job at the Abbey National Building Society in a very similar role to that which she had enjoyed at the Leeds. I was a little surprised that her new manager was so amenable, particularly once he discovered that I worked for a competitor. Sue had obviously made a positive impression. She settled in very quickly and was delighted to make new friends.

BACK UP NORTH

In addition to my trip when returning Jim's somewhat battered Cortina, I enjoyed several more visits to Leeds. It was a pleasure to receive a call from David Wilks the car fleet manager saying that my new Talbot Horizon was ready for collection - even if it was yellow and had its radio removed! Sue and I decided to make the most of the trip by tagging on a couple of days at a B&B in York. We did all the main visitor attractions including the Viking Centre and York Minster. We also found time to pay a very modest fee to inspect an open-air archaeological dig at Coppergate.

With the business year ending on the 30th September the Society's AGM was held at Leeds Town Hall every January. This was an opportunity to invite all managers to attend from both HO and the branches. Overnight accommodation was provided and a formal dinner was held at the Queens Hotel in the centre of the city, a short walk from both HO and the Town Hall.

I was excited to meet up with friends from the Midlands including Andy and Dan who were now managers at Lichfield and Stretford (Manchester) respectively. The dinner was a boozy do as the company was footing the drinks bill. The recently retired Chief General Manager, now President,

Leonard Hyde certainly seemed to have had his fair share prior to taking a tumble down the main hotel staircase. Remarkably he bounced at the bottom and without a moment's pause he stood up as if nothing had happened. There was much singing that night particularly from beyond both the Welsh and Scottish borders.

The next morning there were lots of aching heads trying to concentrate as senior HO staff offered their business presentations. Half way through the morning it was announced that due to worsening weather the Scottish contingent would be released. A whoop went up and chairs were rapidly vacated across the room. No such luck for the rest of us although there was a delicious buffet for those of us whose delicate stomachs were up to the challenge.

In the spring of 1980 I again returned to Leeds to attend a very pleasant awards lunch for successful graduates of The Chartered Building Society Institute. There were eleven of us hosted by the Chief General Manager, Stanley Walker. Three of us, Dan Heaphy, Phil Williams and I, had started our exams with the support of Spiny Norman back in Birmingham in 1976. I was very impressed that Dan had managed to pass all his exams without attending college. There was only one lady graduate attending, Mary Banks from HO Training Department. There were still no female branch managers at that time but there were signs of equality gathering pace with the number of female trainees beginning to grow.

DODGY DEALINGS

As a new Branch Manager I felt it was important to establish my own level of good business conduct. Around Christmas one of our valuers came to see me clutching a bulky envelope which he presented to me. I opened it but on seeing the contents I quickly passed it back. It was common business practice for bottles to be given at Christmas so I suggested that this would be a more acceptable 'gift'. He duly obliged. The staff were always delighted to share in these Christmas gifts.

Our agents were paid a generous commission on investment receipts providing the money stayed invested for at least three months. I kept a careful record of large amounts flowing in and out from our agents and it soon became clear that one of them was taking advantage. Certain customers were withdrawing large amounts after the three months and immediately reinvesting their funds. This would lead to the Society paying four times the commission due in a full year leading to a substantial loss.

I made an appointment to see the agent concerned and went armed with the evidence. Did he deny it? No he maintained it was good business practice and said our figures would be much lower if it stopped. I pointed out that it had to stop or the agency would have to close. He was not happy, but his remarkable "turn over" ceased. The figures reduced but I felt more comfortable knowing that I had done what was right for the business. It is likely that if the customers had been challenged they would have said that they thought they needed the funds, but then changed their minds so decided to reinvest. I am pretty sure similar activity was taking place in other parts of the country, but I was not prepared to turn a blind eye on my patch.

As our mortgage allocation was small prospective mortgage interviews were an infrequent event. One day I was asked to deal with a very irate customer who would not accept that his income was insufficient for the mortgage he was requesting. It was policy that self-employed applicants needed to provide three years' accounts as evidence of their ability to repay. When the irate customer pleaded: "But I earn far more than you can see" I tactfully reminded him that that when applying for a mortgage, he could not have his cake and eat it. He just left in a huff.

HERE COMES THE SUN

During my first year business had grown at a reasonable rather than spectacular rate. I was also pleased to note that the staff were trying their best to make sure customers were aware of appropriate products. Mike was particularly creative with our window displays as well as making sure the plant troughs outside were fully stocked with colourful arrangements.

In addition to summer bedding plants Mike had planted a small conifer at the end of each trough. They were about 3 feet tall and made a nice feature. One morning in the middle of summer we arrived to find soil all over the ground and one of the small conifers partially uprooted. Whilst Mike was tutting away, replacing the soil and straightening the trough a policeman approached. He explained that the previous evening at around 11pm he had spotted a youth running down the street with a conifer in his hand. He turned the corner and collided with another officer. When asked what he was doing the quick thinking lad replied," I found this and as I knew where it had come from I was taking it back". The policeman felt inclined to let him off, possibly fearing the bright lad might accuse him of planting the evidence (I know, I know).

That summer I experienced my first "corporate jolly". A firm of estate agents, Lalonde Bros and Parham, had recently opened in the town and generously invited several local contacts to cricket at the county ground in Taunton. Partners were invited to the John Player Sunday League Limited Overs match featuring Somerset against Yorkshire.

There were about forty of us using a private facility with food and drinks provided. We sat on deck chairs on the grass just outside the bar and enjoyed watching some well know cricketers including Ian Botham, Sunil Gavaskar and Geoffrey Boycott.

Sue wasn't a cricket lover but feigned interest for a while. Before too long, however, the heat of the early summer sun proved too much of a temptation. She slowly shuffled her deck chair round until she had achieved a full 180 degrees and sat facing the sun rather than the match. No one minded, it was a "jolly" and to be enjoyed by everyone. The drinks flowed and the cricket was pretty much forgotten.

A couple of weeks later I was off to cricket again this time with David Ware, our Taunton valuer. David was on the short side, a little chubby and great fun. He had a never-ending supply of jokes. I could have done with his help at that Round Table dinner.

David had invited me for a day trip to Lords, the home of cricket, to experience the first day of the 2nd Test against the powerful West Indies team. We had good seats in the Mound stand and settled down to watch with England winning the toss and electing to bat.

Gooch and Boycott opened the batting to face a hostile pace attack of four seamers headed by Roberts and Holding. Boycott was soon back in the pavilion having been caught by wicketkeeper Murray off Holding. Enter Chris Tavare to support Gooch at the other end. My own batting style was often compared to Tavare: not in ability but in being able to bore onlookers almost to death. He batted nearly all day for his 42 before becoming another wicket for Holding. Gooch had a splendid knock reaching his first Test Match century.

With the odd beer thrown in it was a great day out. The sun never really broke through the cloud but I still managed to head back home with a bright red face.

With the arrival of warmer days Sue and I decided to try out one or two of the local pubs. We both often worked on Saturday mornings, so settled on a bright summer's afternoon to head for our village pub, The Malt Shovel. Not surprisingly cider was very popular in Somerset and Sue was keen to sample the local brew. I had seen the effect it had on some of the locals, particularly those who slept on benches in the town, but had no idea what it was really like.

On arrival we were surprised to find the pub so quiet but we were on a mission and not to be put off. Sue found a table in a corner and I approached the bar. When I asked for a cider for

Sue the barman asked if I wanted 'draught' or 'rough'. In answer to my confused expression he explained that 'rough' was the local homemade variety. I opted for that on a "when in Rome" basis. The barman placed a glass of what could best be described as golden murk. It was more than cloudy, it was dense and had bits floating in it. Nevertheless Sue was keen to give it a try and it was soon downed..... but so was Sue! When we decided to leave she could not stand up without my support. Fortunately, we only lived a couple of minutes' drive away so I poured Sue into the car and made the short distance home in record time.

As it was a lovely sunny day and I decided Sue could sleep it off on a deck chair in the back garden. She was soon in the land of nod, resurfacing a few hours later, more than a little the worse for wear. A situation I took pleasure in describing as 'rough' justice.

MINEHEAD REVISITED

I had only been to the seaside resort of Minehead on one previous occasion when I was requested by HO to make an arrears call in the area. I decided to make full use of the 60-mile round trip by calling in at a couple of solicitors in the town.

I arrived on a lovely bright autumn morning and went to see the solicitors first. I received a warm welcome from one who we had recently dealt with. I then consulted the mortgage file for the arrears visit. I had a copy of the valuation report, which enabled me to find which road it was on. I set off to the seafront expecting to drive straight up to it. I found the road overlooking the Bristol Channel, but couldn't find the house number I was looking for. Where it should have been were a series of flats.

I decided to pop into the nearby shop and make some enquiries. I was lucky that the person behind the counter knew the history of the road and told me that the house I was looking for had been swallowed up by the building of holiday flats a couple of years previously. The good news was that our borrower seemed to own them all.

When I returned to the office I made a full report and sent it off to HO suggesting they give me a ring when they had considered the problem. A couple of days later the call came. Apparently, whilst strange to me, this was not unheard of. They would refer it to our lawyers but the usual outcome was to take no action unless the arrears became very serious as these cases often resolved themselves as this one did with all the arrears soon cleared. I took it as a learning experience notably that just because a property disappears it doesn't necessarily lead to a massive problem.

VISITORS WELCOME

My good friend Andy and I were following parallel life paths. He had been appointed as Branch Manager for the new Lichfield branch just before I moved down to Bridgwater. He married Terri in September, about a month before Sue and I had tied the knot back home in Olton, Solihull. I was honoured to be his best man.

We kept in regular contact and they came down to stay with us for a few days that autumn. Andy had spent many family holidays in his younger days at the seaside resort of Woolacombe. We all enjoyed his guided tour, which included stopping off at Dunster Castle and Lynmouth, the scene of devastating floods in 1952.

We had other regular visits from family and friends and often visited the coastal towns, particularly Lyme Regis. As winter approached Sue and I liked visiting the seaside out of season preferring the lack of holidaymakers filling car parks and overcrowding everywhere.

MATERNITY SWEET

Back at the office there was good news for Carol as her pregnancy was going well. She was unsure if she would come back to work after giving birth and I therefore placed an advert in the local paper for maternity cover. We were lucky to recruit a smashing young girl called Collette. Not tall but with pretty features and lovely personalities that were readily appreciated by everyone. Carol gave birth to a health little one and the new team soon settled down.

It was a difficult time for Collette, as she had to wait a few months before Carol could make her decision but it all worked out well and she became a valued full member of the team.

ON THE BEACH

We were now an effective team trying our hardest to increase the branch results. A new TV advert was launched to push our strapline; "Say the Leeds and You're Smiling". Someone at HO had the idea that if all counter staff wore a sash bearing the strapline it would go down well. It didn't.

The advert was set on a sunny beach with attractive participants frolicking on the sand. The most memorable scene in the advert was a topless girl who, when lying face down on the sand received a cold ice cream dropped on her back. The camera shot away a split second before she completed her rapid turnover.

All staff were instructed to wear the sashes to coincide with the first day of broadcasting. We duly obliged but rather than smiling, our customers were mystified. No one appeared to have seen the infrequently aired ads so the clever marketing strategy was lost on them. It was all a little embarrassing and I readily agreed staff could stop wearing the sashes. The good news was that the strapline stuck for many years.

OPPORTUNITY KNOCKS

As we moved into 1981 my contacts back in the Midlands informed me that the Society had bought premises in the middle of Cannock and a new Leeds branch was due to open in a few months. I had only been in Bridgwater for about 18 months but I was very interested in the prospect of Cannock. I knew the area well, the agency was already as busy as Bridgwater was and would soon be a grade higher. It would also mean that Sue and I would be closer to our families.

No interviews were held for appointments but I decided to take the bull by the horns and ask to be considered for the branch. I drafted out a letter to my Regional Manager Mike Rooke highlighting all the reasons why I was ideally suited for the new position. As Area Rep I had been responsible for the Cannock agency and knew the area well. My performance at Bridgwater had displayed evidence of initiative and sound management. I asked Mike for his support and for him to recommend me to HO.

One evening after the office had closed Sue sat down at a typewriter and said that if she managed to type the long letter with no mistakes I would get the job. She did, and I was appointed.

My time at Bridgwater was a very valuable learning experience. My first management role taught me how to run a branch, recruit staff and motivate a team. I learnt a lot about business ethics and how to make balanced business decisions. I felt ready to take a step up the management ladder that I knew Cannock would offer.

CHAPTER 5
CANNOCK
MAY 1981 TO SEPTEMBER 1983

THE TOWN

Cannock lies off Junction 12 on the M6 where the A5 and A34 meet. Mentioned in The Domesday Book, it reached its economic peak on the back of coal mining in the late 1800s and is now best known as a dormitory area north of the West Midlands conurbation. Cannock has a population of just under 30,000 and is encircled by Wolverhampton to the south east, Stafford to the north, Lichfield to the east, and Walsall to the south, all approximately eleven miles from the town centre.

BACK HOME

I hadn't previously been involved with the opening of a new branch and was excited at the prospect of building my own team in an area I knew well. Whilst still at the Bridgwater branch I had received a call from my new boss, Mike Blades. The Midlands region had grown rapidly in the twenty or so months I had been away and consequently had been divided into two regions, imaginatively named 'Midlands' and 'West Midlands'.

Mike was very enthusiastic about the post and told me to station myself at my old branch in Wolverhampton until the Cannock branch (West Midlands) became operational in a few months' time. My priority was to recruit two cashier typists. Whilst still in Bridgwater I duly placed an advertisement The Express and Star.

I needed to wait a few weeks and hand over to my replacement, Peter Davis, before I could make the journey back up the M5. I left Sue to put our house on the market with our original agent Greenslades. As luck would have it a girl working at Lloyds Bank next to the branch got to hear the house was on the market and she and her husband agreed to buy it almost straight away. Handover complete, house almost sold, Sue left to pack up and I was off.

MORE LIKE BRUM

Malcolm, my old manager at the Wolverhampton branch, gave me a warm welcome and introduced me to the current team, virtually all of whom were new. Since leaving less than two years ago, new branches had opened at Bilston and Wednesfield. They were a new type of branch called sub-branches. Due to their relatively low level of business they came under the management of Malcolm in Wolverhampton. In addition, the long running planning issues at Bridgnorth had been resolved and that branch was now open under the management of Terry Matthews who had replaced me as the rep when I went off to Bridgwater. He was ably assisted by Christine Goodwin. I reflected that with the move to Bridgwater and now Cannock things were turning out well for me.

My branch was due to open in June, with a new branch in Wellington under the direction of Colin Taylor following soon after. His would be the fifth new branch to open in the Wolverhampton patch since I left. Colin was in a similar position to me except he was coming straight from the role of rep. My old branch was packed with staff. It was now fulfilling a similar role to Birmingham, training staff for rapid expansion in the area.

WHERE THERE'S MUCK

I was desperate to get stuck in but my new branch had been an old butchers shop and in need of complete refurbishment. I arranged an onsite meeting with the surveyors in early May but was rather dismayed to discover my shiny new branch was still very much a building site. I was also disappointed by the apparent lack of space. The finish was hard to imagine but it was obviously going to be smaller than any of my previous branches. I couldn't see how it would be finished in time for opening in June.

The good news was its location. Situated right in the middle of the Market Place, it couldn't have been more central. Another huge plus was the lack of competition. None of the big boys were in town, only two local societies: The Staffordshire and The Heart of England. Given the population and the strength of The Leeds agency I was confident that despite being small, the new branch would be a success.

TEAM STARTS TO TAKE SHAPE

I was told that my Chief Clerk would be Bob Adams, one of the management trainees from Wolverhampton. Although I had no say in his appointment, I was delighted. Tall, with fair hair and glasses, Bob was as straight as a dye and as keen as mustard. He was also a passionate support of Wolverhampton Wanderers, but then nobody is perfect.

The response to the adverts for staff was very good, which gave Bob and I a strong shortlist of suitable candidates. There were two applicants that stood out: Sue who worked at the Leeds Agency in Brownhills linked to our Lichfield branch and managed by my good friend Andy Bates; and Yvonne from the Cannock branch of the Staffordshire Building Society. Sue was tall with long brown hair and a friendly approach. This combined with her being familiar with our products and a good cashier ensured that she was a "shoe in". Yvonne was also a very strong candidate; my only concern was why she wanted to work for a competitor. Her explanation was a clash of personality with her manager. I made a few discreet enquiries with our agents located opposite the Staffordshire, and soon gave Yvonne the nod.

Recruiting two new staff with Building Society experience was a real advantage. Sue lived a short bus ride away and Yvonne was within walking distance of our new branch.

HOUSE SEARCH

During my first few weeks in Cannock The Leeds put me up in the very comfortable Mount Hotel. As it was summer the light evenings enabled me to go house hunting after work. Since buying in Somerset, local house prices had risen which put us in a good position for buying in Cannock. I started searching for a detached property in the town.

There was only one really smart area in Cannock itself but that was out of our price range. I found a very nice three bedroom detached house on the other side of Cannock Chase in the small market town of Rugeley. When I mentioned this to colleagues back at Wolverhampton there was a sharp intake of breath and shaking of heads. I was told that the house might be nice but there were much better areas to consider. I crossed it off my list.

My pal Andy introduced me to one of his insurance contacts, a guy called Steve Bostock. I immediately referred to him as 'Ole Biscuit Barrel' after the Monty Python character ' Bostock F'tang, F'tang Ole Biscuit Barrel, representative of The Silly Party'. (Apologies to those not familiar with Monty Python). Steve lived on the developing Boley Park estate in Lichfield and suggested I take a look. To my surprise there was a house for sale in the next road to Steve that was identical to the one in Rugeley. Sue came up to view it and after a brief discussion the deal was sealed. Andy and Terri lived in the village of Whittington just three miles to the east of Lichfield making the move to Boley Park even more enticing.

CAR WARS

Colin Taylor, a former teacher and now the prospective manager of the soon to be opened Wellington branch was married to Ina, also a former teacher and now a successful author. She had recently published a biography of the author of "The Country Diary of an Edwardian Lady" and sales were rocketing.

Colin was technically still a rep at Wolverhampton but had been replaced by Guy Fenny who I knew from my time at the Birmingham branch. Colin had thin lips, a body to match and a very wide parting. He was a confident chap who announced at our first meeting that his aim was to become our Chief Executive. As he was only a few years older than me, although not as experienced, I thought this was more than a little optimistic. As a rep he was still driving a dark brown Mini 850.

Ina was working on her next book and planned to spend a week researching in the West Country accompanied by Colin and their young daughter. Colin approached me about a car swap for the trip. He pointed out that my Talbot Horizon was bigger and more suitable for family holidays than his tiny two door underpowered Mini. I was not overjoyed at the prospect of bumping about in his Mini but felt I couldn't refuse.

That week seemed like a month to me but Colin told me it had been a very worthwhile trip. When we swapped the cars back Colin thanked me and I politely waited for him to pass over a little something, a stick of rock at the very least, but nothing was forthcoming. I didn't even get a copy of the book when it came out.

CUPBOARD LOVE

By the end of May I was getting impatient to move in to the new branch. The builders had moved out and the shop fitters were nearing completion so we weren't far off. However, my final meeting with the HO surveyor revealed quite how restricted we were on space. I was shocked by the size of the Manager's office. The surveyor did his best to reassure me that a desk and three chairs would fit comfortably. He rolled out some of the wallpaper that would line the walls and enthusiastically drew my attention to the trees on the paper claiming it would deepen the perspective and make the room seem larger. Nice try but it was obvious that I was moving from the "black hole of Bridgwater" to a "cupboard in Cannock". When the furniture arrived Bob and I just about managed to fit two customer chairs opposite the smallest desk I had ever seen. That left just enough room for my chair and NOTHING else. No natural light and one door. It was a cupboard, and I didn't love it.

DAY ONE

Training with Yvonne and Sue had gone well in Wolverhampton and with a last minute scramble to unpack the numerous boxes of stationery we were all set to begin business.

We opened the door to our first new customers on June 15th 1981. I presented the usual flowers and whisky with Bob taking photos for the local press and the in-house 'Leeder' paper. Over the next few days customers flowed through the door and we knew that the branch was heading for success.

CHANGES

Away from Cannock, The Leeds was progressing. The first female Branch Managers were appointed at West Bromwich, and at Acomb near York. Their appointment date on 1st April was a little unfortunate but still a sure sign of progress. Even the thought of allowing beards had grown on the powers that be.

Sponsorship of the RLSS (Royal Life Saving Society) was announced. Our most obvious link to the RLSS was the launch of the Leeds swimbag. They were ideal for carrying swim wear and towels and had the Leeds logo at one end of the cylindrical bag with the RLSS logo at the other end. The bags were often given away with the opening of new accounts and were soon seen across the country and on many beaches. Our "go ahead" Regional Manager Mike Blades was keen to make the most of the link and decided to use a good chunk of the recently provided regional marketing budget on the purchase of a caravan. This was good news for the region as it proved to be an attractive focal point at shows and fairs. It was not such good news for me as it was stored in our car park behind the branch. Thankfully I wasn't given responsibility for moving it about, this task was delegated to other managers with experience of towing caravans.
For many months it was successfully used to promote both the

RLSS and The Leeds. However, the end came one evening as it was being towed home along the busy A38 after a show. The caravan suddenly began to swing from side to side and unfortunately this particular driver was not sufficiently experienced in caravan towing to realise that he needed to accelerate to correct the swing. Instead he slowed down, the van swung wildly, broke free and took off, finally coming to rest in a collapsed heap by the side of the road. Thankfully no one was hurt, and better still, our car park returned to normal.

My new boss was full of new ideas. He introduced various committees to focus on areas such as training, marketing and social events. To aid development and involvement he set up a club for Managers to invest £10 a month to buy shares. A local stockbroker was invited along and I volunteered to chair the newly formed WEMRIC (West Midlands Regional Investment Club). We focused on very low priced shares such as the mining company Endeavour Resources. We didn't make much money but we had fun and learnt a lot.

Mike was very keen on setting up savings schemes for both schools and companies. I didn't really share his enthusiasm. School schemes were time consuming and necessarily a long term bet and there were very few potential   companies in our area. I did, however, agree to deliver the odd talk and explain the role of building societies and the importance of saving to kids who either had no money to save or a greater desire to spend it on sweets. Eventually Mike accepted that the scope for setting up saving schemes in Cannock was extremely limited.

Although Mike was not himself a member of the Building Societies Institute, he was keen to support membership. There was a group of building society people who wanted to establish a Building Societies Institute local centre in Walsall and before I knew it I was elected Chairman of the committee and working hard to get it off the ground.

ON THE RIGHT TRACK

In August 1981, after a hectic summer, Sue and I took a break in Majorca. Immediately on our return we moved into our new home in Lichfield. We were very pleased with the house but had a bit of a surprise when we retired exhausted on our first night. The weather was very warm so we had left most of the windows open. As we lay in bed the rattling of trains seemed to be coming at us from all directions. We knew there was a seldom used goods line about 50 yards behind the house, but we hadn't realised that there were two main lines converging on the far side of the estate. The noise seemed to carry on the summer evening air but as the weather cooled and our senses adapted we soon forgot about the trains.

There was good news on the job front for Sue as Spiny, the Midlands Regional Manager, welcomed her back to work for The Leeds at the in-store branch located in the Carrefour hypermarket at Minworth. The branch was really just a very busy counter operating under the Erdington manager, Paul Squires. The Leeds was also experimenting with this type of facility at one of the car factories with similar success.

Sue loved being back at the Leeds and working with many of the staff she knew from a couple of years ago. It was shift work and not full time but it suited Sue.

FREE LUNCH

It was common practice to celebrate the opening of a new branch with a lunch or dinner organised by the Business Operations department at HO. The main purpose was to mark the occasion by inviting representatives of the local business community to meet the new manager and to enjoy the company of senior managers from Head Office and Directors.

When our turn came we searched for an appropriately smart local venue. The Hollies restaurant was far too small. A new hotel had recently opened close to the M6 just outside Cannock. Bob and I went to have a close look at the Roman Way Hotel on Watling Street. To our surprise it was quite modern with the only 'Roman' reference restricted to a couple of columns at the entrance. It lacked class and was not really large enough so was crossed off the list. Finding nothing suitable in the Cannock area, the dinner was instead hosted at the Mount Hotel in Wolverhampton.

Fifty guests joined eleven Leeds directors and senior managers for a very pleasant dinner one evening in November. Surprisingly a third of the guests had travelled down from Stafford. Despite this being the county town there was a total lack of representation from The Leeds, a rather obvious gap. I don't think I saw any of the Stafford set again.

TABLING

I soon made one or two good local business contacts. I hit it off with a young solicitor who worked for a successful firm located just around the corner. We had started to do business together and I had taken him to The Hollies restaurant for lunch. He reciprocated by inviting me to a Rotary dinner. I readily accepted.

My knowledge of Rotary was limited to thinking it was a bit like a more serious version of Round Table but with no age limit. I was instructed to wear an evening suit and was informed the dinner had a sports theme.

I knew the drinks would flow so booked a taxi to take me home at the end of the night. I was looking forward to an enjoyable evening where I didn't have to stand up and tell jokes, as I had at the Round Table do in Bridgwater. I was anticipating a relaxing time with sensible, even a little old fashioned, folk. I was in for a shock.

The meal was very good, and the company friendly. I asked my host what the sport element was, and he told me just to wait and see, as all would be revealed in time.

I became more curious when a large curtain was pulled back to reveal the other half of the room where four table tennis tables stood. Aha! So this was the sports angle. The Rotary chairman stood in front of tables and read out the names of four pairs of players, which included myself and my host. We were on Table 1. I thought it strange that we were playing singles, but each pair were instructed to stay at one end and await the entrance of the "professionals". Oh no I thought, this could be even more humiliating than having to tell a joke in public.

I had been warned that all would be revealed, and moments later it was. Eight TOPLESS, yes topless, ladies entered the room. Dressed in tuxedos and bow ties, but missing the obvious undergarments, the only clue that they were there to play table tennis was that they arrived with bat in hand. I could not believe it. In fact I still can't. My impression of Rotary changed in a flash. Feeling very uncomfortable and not quite knowing what to do I told myself to keep my eye on the ball!

To be honest the idea did not work on any level. The ladies had been put in a very difficult position. It was clear that they were not proficient players and were embarrassed by their lack of skill. Every chap played but 'game over' did not come soon enough for most of us and predictably the evening tailed off. I never went to another Rotary do, politely making excuses to my host although we continued to do plenty of business.

BOB'S YOUR UNCLE

Business continued to flourish, and the following summer Chief Clerk Bob was ready to launch his career as an Area Rep. He was very efficient and excellent with customers. One day he was chatting away with a customer when suddenly the lady turned quite serious and said, "You know what really gets my goat?" Bob politely replied "No" and braced himself for a complaint about the branch. The lady paused, drew a deep breath, and declared "Squashed bread niggles me". I would have corpsed on the spot but Bob calmly stood back and agreed that indeed squashed bread was one of life's more difficult problems.

After successfully passing his reps' interview with Jack Clark at HO, Bob received a call from Regional Office offering him a position in Chelmsford. Not surprisingly he hesitated for two main reasons: the cost of living in the south, and the distance from his beloved Wolves FC (as well as his family and friends).

The pace of branch openings was slowing and after much thought he took the role. I was pleased for Bob but knew it would be a challenge for him and his fiancee Kim. I was, however, delighted to welcome Alan Jones as his replacement and not just because he was a Villa fan. At about six feet five "big Al" was the regional football team's goalkeeper and also a very effective Chief Clerk.

BUSINESS ACCELERATES

The business results continued on an upward trend and we soon needed another member of staff. My old boss Malcolm told me that one of his previous counter staff who had left to have children was looking to return part-time. I got in contact and Judy quickly became one of the team. She was soon back in the swing as little had changed on the counter apart from having to key counter sheets into the dumb terminal (well it never answered back!). Judy, Sue and Yvonne worked well together and I felt we were a happy branch.

I was enjoying my role as Manager and particularly liked writing press releases and obtaining coverage in the local free paper. We had good support from the local solicitors and estate agents. All was going well until we heard on the grapevine that competition was coming to town. A rival building society had been granted planning permission to open a new branch. Towards the end of that year the Anglia opened for business, and as it turned out wasn't really much of a threat. The branch was situated at the far end of the town centre and the only thing I envied was the much larger manager's office. What I definitely didn't envy was the press coverage the manager received when it was alleged that he had revealed more than he should have to a group of young girls waiting at the bus stop beneath his bedroom window.

We needn't have worried about the competition as our business was unaffected and continued to thrive.

AND ONE MAKES THREE

Sue enjoyed being back with The Leeds but didn't last very long in the job. That summer we found out she was expecting our first child, due at Christmas. The pregnancy went well and all was set for our own nativity.

With Sue heavily pregnant and Christmas approaching Steve Bostock (F'tang F'tang etc) who lived in the next road invited Andy and I to a memorable cricket event.

England were playing in an Ashes series in Australia and it was on terrestrial TV for the very first time. It started at close to midnight by which time Steve had made sure we had more than just sampled his home brew. Worse still by the time fast bowler Norman Cowans had launched the first red ball I was ready for a different kind of launch. I must have been affected by the home brew as I ended up drinking brandy which I normally dislike and never drink.

We passed through Christmas without any excitement and as New Year approached Sue was taken in to Good Hope Hospital to be monitored. I watched pro-celebrity golf alone on New Year's Eve and was amused to discover that golfer Greg Norman who had just announced the birth of his daughter, decided to call her Morgan. Yes, Morgan Norman. I vowed that our child would have a 'normal' name. After just one hour in labour, at 1pm on New Year's Day Stephen James Duffin was welcomed to the world. As he was one of the first babies to be born in 1983 Sue and Stephen were pictured on the front page of the Lichfield Mercury.

RIVALLING MRS MALAPROP

The financial half-year occurred at the end of March making the branch very busy with interest being credited to many accounts. It was also time for a regional meeting of all West Midland managers. They were always both informative and enjoyable. There were two branches in Walsall town centre. John Rootham, who lacked stature but not opinions, managed the main branch. This senior Branch Manager was locally renowned for his ability to distort the Queen's English. At the meeting Mike asked how the influx of half yearly statements was affecting branches. John immediately sounded off saying that Walsall had been "absolutely unindated". As we giggled silently I thought of asking him if he could be more "pacific" but decided not to embarrass him further. His other favourite phrase was "to all intensive purposes" His English wasn't perfect, but boy could he tow a caravan.

DISTRACTIONS

The Falklands war began on 2nd April and almost at the same time the Ideal Homes exhibition began at the Birmingham National Exhibition Centre. The Leeds decided to take a stand at the exhibition to promote the opening of new accounts. Each new account holder was rewarded with a calculator bearing the Leeds logo.
Leeds employees from all over both the Midlands and West Midlands regions were called in to staff the stand, covering back-to-back shifts. It was pressurised selling, but we only had to work a four hour shift and we had plenty of time to have a good look around the huge exhibition. We also benefitted from the provision of M&S outfits, which we were allowed to keep. This pleased me, although I'm not sure why as I never wore it again. There were usually half a dozen of us on duty at any one time. 'Knocker' Powell from Birmingham Temple Row acted as a very competent supervisor.

As Andy and I lived near each other we tried to work the same shifts in order to share the driving. In the time we were there hundreds of accounts were opened but it was difficult to judge the success of the promotion as a very high percentage of those only ever contained the minimum opening balance of three pounds (to gain the calculator).

It was a strange period. Following the progression of the war in the South Atlantic was disturbing and perhaps our unusual working pattern became a welcome distraction.

GAME CHANGER

You need a bit of luck to progress in a corporate structure. My appointment to Cannock was certainly a very fortunate move and after about twenty months a couple of other events conspired to aid my progression.

I received a call from my boss Mike Blades inviting me to attend a new four-day management training course in Leeds. I responded enthusiastically and a few days later I received three books and was instructed to read them before the course started. One was "The Effective Executive" by Peter Drucker. I can't remember the others but know that I read them all, making notes as I went along. The course was interesting and relatively informative, but I was surprised to discover that of the six of us I seemed to be the only one to have done the pre-course reading. I don't think any of the others had attempted to even familiarise themselves with the course content. This probably made me look far more capable than I deserved. The feedback from the Training Manager, made it difficult for me to get my head through the door.

What I didn't realise at the time was that the training coincided with a decision to introduce promotional interviews for the first time. Hull Paragon Street, a high grade branch was to be the first to benefit from the new approach. Ted Germaine, the General Manager, had suggested that one of my fellow managers should be put forward for interview from the region, but Mike argued that it should be me. Since I had performed well on the recent course, Ted agreed.

Hull Paragon Street was one of the oldest branches in the country. It had been open for sixty years but had only ever had two managers: Joe Barber and Dennis Thornton. Joe had been retired for over 20 years but was still active in the town, as he owned and managed a number of properties. Apparently, in years gone by, staff had been encouraged to purchase repossessed houses, which resulted in a few lucky HO staff being able to develop a portfolio.

I prepared thoroughly and the interview went well. The call confirming my appointment soon followed. Just a few weeks before leaving Cannock I was delighted to learn that my current boss was being promoted to a senior position at HO. This was good news except for the fact that his replacement was being moved from another regional management post. His was not a promotion. I felt lucky to be leaving but felt sorry for Andy and the rest of the region.

I only met Mike's replacement a couple of times but could not believe some of the claims he made. They were so outlandish I could hardly keep a straight face. He famously boasted that he had invented both bingo and the pedal bin but that his ideas had been 'stolen'. He also claimed to have beaten at least one world champion at snooker. His claims may have been true but I felt that moving when I did I had a very lucky escape!

In a matter of weeks, I was heading north on the road to Hull leaving Colin Kemp to take over the new Walsall branch of the Chartered Institute and Steve Maskrey to run Cannock branch. For a short time I also left Sue holding the baby.

WHAT HAD I LEARNT

In addition to experiencing all that opening a new branch entails, I had developed many new skills including chairmanship and how to make full use of the local press. Mike Blades had been a great coach and mentor encouraging me to try new things. I also learnt to take all opportunities seriously and volunteer to take on new roles. I felt that I was really making headway.

CHAPTER 6
HULL PARAGON STREET
SEPTEMBER 1983 TO NOVEMBER 1985

THE CITY

Hull lies in the East Riding of Yorkshire at the confluence of the rivers Hull and Humber. Founded in the 12th century it has been both a trading and fishing port. Despite the decline of the fishing industry in the 1970s it is still a busy port, with the ferry terminal supporting more than one million passengers a year. The resident population of over 250,000 relies heavily on the health and chemical industries. A recent addition to industry is the Siemens Wind Power base at Alexander Dock.

Hull is infamous for having cream telephone boxes originally installed by Kingston Communications in 1914 and maintained by them to this day. A more prestigious accolade for Hull was the award for City of Culture in 2017.

DAY ONE

I met my new boss Mike Gunson, the Yorkshire Regional Manager who was based above our branch of the Leeds in the attractive town of Harrogate. He had a passing resemblance for the comedian Ronnie Barker although he had a strong Yorkshire accent and was not quite as funny. In fact he was pretty bluff. I did not receive a warm welcome and he got straight down to business, "I want you to get me three school saving schemes and a similar number of company ones". I listened and respectfully acknowledged his demands, without any intention of putting saving schemes at the top of my priorities. The branch had tremendous savings balances but was relatively low on mortgage business. Whilst Mike probably felt under pressure to be seen to be supporting the flavour of the month, I had decided that mortgages were going to be my immediate priority.

Mike briefly gave me a run down on the staff, paying particular attention to the Area Rep Phil Harriman who he knew well and rated highly. There were two branches in Hull: my new home in Paragon Street, and the smaller Storey Street branch managed by Dave Ellis. Mike referred to the large imposing Dave as "WEBBO" apparently from a beer commercial for Webster's Yorkshire bitter. The reference went straight over my head. I was beginning to think the 70-mile division between my new boss and Hull would become a great advantage.

An hour and a half after leaving Harrogate I arrived in the centre of Hull and parked at the railway station not far from the branch. A scrawl of graffiti greeted me on the station wall proclaiming, "Arthur Scargill should be bloody well hung". Underneath someone had added, "HE IS!" followed by Mrs Scargill's signature. It was a pleasing introduction to the local sense of humour.

SIZE MATTERS

I knew that my new office was huge by Leeds standards so I was keen to be given the tour. Situated on a corner site, it had six tills and two internal offices. The manager's office could have swallowed both my Bridgwater and Cannock offices at least twice over. It had a large frosted window down one side, and doors to both the front and back offices. A real palace! The only let down to the whole building was the staff kitchen and rest area that turned out to be small, dark and not very handsome.

Being responsible for eleven staff was going to be a huge leap from managing just four at the Cannock branch. My first impression was that there was a good mix of youth and experience. The rep, Phil, had not been there long but was enthusiastic and had the respect of the staff. He introduced me to everyone in turn. The old-fashioned title of "Chief Clerk" had now been updated to become "Assistant Branch Manager (ABM)", a role ably filled by David Fox who, although quiet, appeared to be confident. Jean was our longest serving staff member. She was a full time cashier and had been with the branch for ten years or more. There were two trainees, Mark Roden and Neil Brown. Neil had joined straight from school which was unusual as trainees were more often recruited after they had gained experience elsewhere. Mark had evidently been at the branch for a while and was due for promotion. Of the girls, Deidre, was the most experienced and was mainly involved with mortgage processing. Angela and Christine were primarily focused on covering counter duties, leaving Judy and Alison as the cashier/typists. As I was introduced, I told them all that I would take a few days to assess the operation before making any changes, and promised an open discussion where their views would be welcomed.

TIME FOR CHANGE

Having worked at two similar sized branches namely, Birmingham Temple Row and Wolverhampton, I had seen how to organise large branches to achieve maximum impact on business.

The counter was extremely busy and relied on a combination of full time cashiers, cashier typists and trainees. The profile of customers appeared to be skewed towards older females. We did not seem to be attracting younger people such as the many local office staff, which was surprising given our city centre location. I realised that a change to the customer profile would be important if I was to increase our mortgage business.

One issue stood out; the lunchtime rota. Although not a high priority for the business, I was amazed to see that all staff took an hour and a quarter for lunch often making cover for the counter problematic. Apparently this was a throwback to the days when Head Office (HO) staff were given this generous concession. Both previous mangers came from HO and therefore probably brought this with them.

I decided that the lunch breaks needed to be normalised but a "quid pro quo" would be offered. I contacted HO surveyors and asked if they would be able to help improve the pokey staff rest area. I was delighted that they readily agreed to come over to Hull and develop some options.

I only waited a few days before holding my first team meeting. I explained the need to increase mortgage business and encourage younger customers. I was pleased by the flow of ideas to move things forward, such as local promotions aimed at attracting younger people. Someone suggested linking up with the local commercial radio station. I quickly made a note of this interesting idea.

When it came to what I thought would be the difficult topic of lunch breaks the reduction to one hour sailed through. I finished the meeting with the news that the staff area was to be refurbished and was gratified by the genuine appreciation and even some excitement.

NOT PARTICULARLY PC

I wanted to introduce some new blood to refresh the team. The management trainee, Mark was soon promoted to a new role as ABM at the Chester branch. He was quickly followed by Alison's departure. I was very keen to bring in two bright, outgoing and enthusiastic recruits. I gave the task to Phil, enabling him to gain some useful recruitment experience. I know it is not PC these days but my brief to Phil was that we needed people with great customer and administrative skills, and it would help if they were also physically attractive! Tut Tut I hear you cry, but this was 1984.

Phil recruited Julia and Sally. Both girls were in their early twenties, smart and yes, they were also attractive. Putting their attractiveness to one side they had great all round skills and were easily the strongest candidates. In just a few weeks they had become real assets to the team and their enthusiasm was infectious.

ERIC THE VIKING

We were soon looking for ways of attracting more young

people through the door. One of our younger customers was a presenter on Viking Radio, the local commercial station. I got chatting to him one day and asked if he was interested in putting together a joint promotion that would benefit us both. Together we devised a competition featuring Eric the Viking, a fictitious character already used by the station, asking pop questions during a Sunday morning programme. As I had managed to acquire half a dozen Sony Walkmans from Head Office the competition naturally ran for six weeks with the winning contestant being awarded a Walkman as a prize each week. It was a success for both Viking FM and us.

I was interviewed at both the launch of the competition and at its conclusion five weeks later. I gained valuable radio experience, the Leeds got increased exposure and Viking listening figures rose – win, win.

A few days after the launch I was sitting in my office when the head cashier (a promotion for Jean) came in to tell me that a young man was at the counter and was convinced he knew me. Curious, I went out to greet him but struggled to recognise him at first. He smiled and as soon as he spoke I realised that it was Tim Yardley a family friend from home who I hadn't seen for a long time.

The Yardleys were close friends from Birmingham, my hometown and my brother and I had spent much of our youth in their company. Tim explained that he was at Hull University on a business studies course and had heard me on Viking Radio. We chatted away catching up on family news. I could not resist telling him the true story his mum, the lovely Eileen (mackintosh supplier from chapter one) had delighted in telling my Mum when they helped out at a local playgroup. When Tim was about three or four years old he was looking out of the lounge window when he started to get really excited and shouted to his mum, "The Duffins are coming, the Duffins are coming!". Eileen was not expecting us and ran to the window. She laughed when she saw that it was the 'dustbin' men, not the Duffins marching up the drive.

I was more than ten years older than Tim so growing up I had spent more time with his older sisters, Jane and Anne. We enjoyed some time recounting old tales and sharing news of our respective families and Tim brought me up to date with his cousins Joy and Richard who were my next door neighbours when I was growing up. I was delighted that Tim had sought me out and we were able to relive some precious memories of these lovely families.

OUT WEST

Back in the Midlands our house in Lichfield sold quickly and Sue and I decided to look for a house on Hull's west side as I had heard there were some very nice villages in the area. It would also make travelling in to town much easier. We soon found a modern four bed detached property in North Ferriby just eight miles from the city centre.

As Stephen was coming up to his first birthday it was natural for Sue to make friends with other local mothers. Julie and Sue quickly became friends. Thirty something years on, Julie still lives in the village and she and Sue are still in touch.

IT'S NOT WHAT YOU KNOW

Phil was a great rep. He knew everyone worth knowing in the business community. He was still in his twenties, divorced from his first wife and now playing the field. It was claimed that when he eventually left Hull to manage his own branch, his little black book was auctioned off at a high price.

There is a narrow street in Hull known as "the land of green ginger". It is there that you can find The George. We often did find it as did many of the city's professionals. It was a time when people still drank at lunchtimes. I usually let Phil take the strain but would often turn out on busy Fridays when many celebrated POETS day (P**S Off Early Tomorrow's Saturday).

One person who was almost part of the furniture at The George was my colleague from the other Leeds branch, manager Dave 'WEBBO' Ellis. Dave was a big lad who had an unquenchable thirst. His sizable frame and love of best bitter led him to be known as 'WEBBO' after the giant in the Websters Yorkshire bitter TV advertisements. The catch phrase was "Watch out for Webbo". We didn't need to because he was a lovely lad with a ready smile and a kind nature.

Phil had a strong relationship with many of the professional contacts particularly with solicitor firms such as Lockings (Andrew Locking and Bill Rispin) and Payne and Payne (Patrick Craft). Good estate agency connections had been made with Hubbards at one end of the market, and Larards at the more up-market end. These connections would prove vital in the pursuit of increased mortgage business.

CRICKET TURNS TO HOCKEY

As my first summer in Hull arrived I was asked by my boss Mike Gunson if I would like to invite a couple of business contacts to watch a day's cricket at the Headingley ground in Leeds, the home of Yorkshire cricket. I readily accepted and decided that Phil and I would take a couple of our solicitor contacts. I invited Patrick Craft (Pat) and Phil invited Simon Escreet.

I opted to drive as they were our guests and I did not want to drink. The weather was fine until we left the M62. By the time we got to the ground the rain was tumbling down. My boss welcomed us as we entered the pavilion. There were thirty or more Leeds' managers and guests enjoying the free bar.

As we looked out on the increasingly wet outfield all we could see was the odd person, mainly players in their whites, walking around the edge of the playing surface heading for the betting tent. As I looked at the leaden sky I thought the only bet worth placing would be on there being no play.

It was decided to bring the formal lunch forward which meant more alcohol for everyone except the drivers. It rapidly became apparent that Simon had spent our first hour there very much enjoying the free bar. As we ate our lunch the rain eased, but Simon's intake didn't. By the time play was abandoned he, and many other guests, were well passed caring if there was any cricket as long as the drinks kept coming.

I drove back to Hull and was astonished that Simon insisted on being taken to his Hockey Club at Welton for continued drinking. The only good news was that Welton was only a couple of miles from Ferriby which enabled me to leave my car there and have a couple of well deserved drinks and arrange for a taxi to take us home. The next day Simon referred to it as "a great day". Phil and I were just amazed he could remember any of it.

TWICE AS NICE

Over the next few months Sue and I settled into Yorkshire life. It wasn't long before we discovered that Sue was expecting again. When the first scan was due I took the afternoon off to look after Stephen who was now seventeen months old.

Following the scan Sue took the opportunity to visit the supermarket on the way back from Beverley Hospital. Arriving home she dropped off the shopping in the kitchen and I helped her unpack. As I stood on the bench to reach a high cupboard I naturally asked how the scan had gone. There were no pictures in those days but Sue wordlessly passed me some paper work and asked me to read it. I read out "multigravida" which apparently meant 'older' mother's second child. "Read on" Sue urged. All I can remember is the word "TWINS" and trying desperately not to fall off the bench. I somehow managed to steady myself and stood silently for a moment whilst letting the message sink in.

Over the next few months Sue had spells of bed rest and my Mum and Sue's parents took it in turns to stay and help look after Stephen until the big day. During one of her spells in hospital I bought Sue a Sony Walkman to help mask the noises coming from the adjacent delivery suite. It was not just the pain-induced yells, but the swearing that reverberated around the whole wing.

As scheduled Sue arranged to go into hospital on a Sunday evening with the birth to be induced the following morning. As instructed I rang the hospital at 8.30am and was informed that Sue was sitting up in bed having breakfast. I packed my sandwiches and filled a flask full of coffee and set off fully prepared for what I thought would be a long day. The drive to Beverley took about thirty minutes.

As I entered the ward two nurses greeted me, each cradling a new-born baby. One wrapped in a pink shawl, the other in blue. "A boy and a girl!" I announced excitedly. "No, two girls" came the reply. The whole thing had lasted less than an hour. Sue had coped admirably but she was a bit miffed not to have been allowed the epidural she was promised.

We had decided on the names in advance leading me to ask Sue which one was Jenna (we can never remember if the name came from the girl in Blake's Seven or the character in Dallas), and which was Sarah. "This is Jenna, and this is Claire" Sue declared with a smile.

By now I was in a daze. First I had missed the births; then I had mistakenly thought we had a boy and a girl; and now the names had changed. My head was in a whirl for a while but it soon passed and I settled with Sue and the girls to enjoy the moment.

They twins had arrived three weeks early and therefore had to stay in hospital for a couple of weeks to put on weight and learn to feed effectively. Eventually when they came home we brought the girls downstairs for Stephen to meet them. He greeted them with the firm scowl of "Back, back!" It was not easy for us to settle into a routine but between them our fantastic parents supported us for most of the next twelve months.

TOY APPEAL AND BLANKET COVERAGE

Soon after the girls' arrival in November, HO announced a joint appeal with Calendar the Yorkshire television programme. All the Leeds' branches in the area became collection points for toys to be given to underprivileged children at Christmas.

We were all very excited when we learnt that the TV crew would be coming to interview staff and customers. I was interviewed by Chris the presenter and told him of my interest in toys now that I had three children under the age of two. Unfortunately, I was edited out, but it was a good experience and everyone at the branch enjoyed the visit.

The toy appeal was soon followed by an appeal to respond to the food crisis in Africa. The Leeds organised a huge collection of blankets to help support the starving masses against the cold nights.

Hull played a key part in the blanket appeal as many of them were shipped from its docks. This provided another radio opportunity to both promote blanket donations and explain the important role of Hull as a port. During the interview I mentioned one somewhat bizarre donation we had received: an electric blanket! The interviewer was left dumbstruck, but it was a good plug for the appeal.

SEEING THE BIGGER PICTURE

The local Building Society Institute (CBSI) was well supported and I was pleased to be appointed chairman. The position opened a few doors for me and gave me valuable networking opportunities.

Unlike the Institute, the Building Societies Association (BSA) was the voice of its members. It provides information to societies and helps them run their businesses. The BSA contacted me about a couple of housing issues. The first was a scheme known as "enveloping". This was mainly a way of improving the outside appearance and therefore attractiveness of properties. I was invited to join BBC Radio Humberside and explain the benefits this would bring to housing in the area. It didn't go too well as both the interviewer and myself became a little confused as to what the limits of "enveloping" were I learnt a valuable lesson in making sure my preparation was thorough enough to cover all eventualities. We did our best and the interview can't have been all bad because the BSA were soon back asking for my services.

HATTON'S GARDENS

The BSA quickly came back via HO asking me to attend a tour of new council housing in Liverpool. At the time the deputy leader of Liverpool City Council was Derek Hatton, a member of the left wing Militant Tendency. The council had launched an urban regeneration scheme including plans to build 5000 new council homes. As soon as the first new houses were completed Hatton organised a coach tour to visit the site in an attempt to convince selected parties such as the BSA, bankers and architects of the merits of the scheme.

This rather sceptical group met at the town hall and after an introduction and refreshments we boarded a coach. Hatton was joined by the head of the council's finance who had been drafted in to help answer our questions. My brief was pretty loose, just to report back on the scheme.

The houses were good examples of modern developments. They all had front and back gardens, which Hatton said was important for children to play in. No arguments there. However it got interesting when the financial numbers were revealed. When asked how much they cost to build, the reported numbers were way above the price the private sector would be able to market similar properties. My feedback was simple: the houses were fine, but the cost looked out of line. The council representatives did not seem to have any problem with the high cost. Far from it, they were proud of what they had achieved. It wasn't long after our visit that the whole scheme collapsed with an embarrassed Hatton expelled from the

Labour party. Interestingly he later became a property developer, amongst other things.

UPPING A GEAR

Technology was beginning to make an impact at the Leeds. As Hull was one of the branches with large savings balances and number of accounts, we were chosen to host an ATM (Automated Teller Machine) better known as a cash dispenser. Although the branch had a large banking hall its design forced the ATM to be sited in an open area. This meant that whenever the machine had to be opened for cash replenishment or removing cheque deposits we had to close the whole branch. This was frankly a pain but there was no alternative.

The need for an ATM was debatable, as the Leeds did not offer customers a current account. The nearest we had to one was our Pay and Save account. This provided a standing order facility, but lacked the key requirement of a current account, namely a chequebook. The ATM was branded "Moneybox" and the cards "Moneycard". We were offering an inferior product that never really made an impact with customers despite being supported by a rather nice (and very durable) leather wallet. I still use one of them.

The ATM was quickly followed by the introduction of a real game changer, Counter Top Terminals (or CTTs as they became known). All passbooks would now have a magnetic strip on the back, which could only be read by the machines on each till. They could also print details of each transaction in the passbook and send the details to the main computers at HO. This meant that there would be no more adding up and keying in at the end of the day. This was a huge benefit much appreciated by the staff.

The installation programme was rolled out across the entire network taking several months. All passbooks had to be changed over and staff had to be suitably trained. The trainers spent several days with us and Phil was happy to look after the young ladies. The introduction of the CTTs marked the end of my exposure to till work partly because I had not been on a till since arriving in Hull and partly because as I paid very little attention to the training. No doubt my retirement from tills helped control the number of cash differences (cash balances) in the branch.

KITCHEN TABLE PROCESSING

After several months of concentrating on stimulating mortgage business, our efforts started to pay off. However the actual administrative process changed at this point which meant more of the underwriting was carried out at branch level rather than merely posting the papers to HO. To ensure the quality of underwriting was up to scratch a weekly error list was issued for the region revealing the number of cases processed and the number and type of errors suffered.

The significant uplift in business at the same time as the change in processing put a great deal of pressure on the team. So much so that Phil and I retreated to my kitchen table in North Ferriby to avoid distractions and work through the pile of applications. I know it is a bit sad but I can still remember the number of the conditions we needed to circle for the repayment of an existing Leeds mortgage, i.e number 45.

OVER THE COUNTER

Now into my second year at Hull things were progressing nicely on all fronts. The team were really performing and business results were ahead of expectation. All was well, or so I thought.

One Monday morning I was sitting in my office reflecting on how well things were going when an almighty noise emanated from the interview room next door. My first thought was that we were being raided and a robbery was in progress. Without thinking I headed for the source of the commotion, (incidentally this is exactly what NOT to do if there is a robbery, we were supposed to observe and be in a position to raise an alarm). I found two men in the interview room growling at each other, arms flailing, being physically separated by Phil. One was a member of staff (name withheld), and the other was a stranger who had apparently leapt over the counter and tried to attack the member of staff.

The cause of the commotion soon became clear as the stranger shouted that our colleague was having an affair with his wife, who also worked at the branch. Said damsel was now in great distress witnessing her husband and lover fighting. We managed to calm both parties down and I took the husband through to my office. I had been totally unaware of the "affair" as I think most of the staff had been too. Fortunately (from my management perspective) I soon had an opportunity to move one of them on to another branch, quickly followed by the other moving on of their own accord.

The whole episode made me think about a lot of things, not least branch security, particularly the lack of "bandit screens" These are now installed in many branches and would have prevented the angered husband's leap over the counter.

On the matter of security we did receive a letter from one customer who seriously suggested we install a series of trap doors in front of each till. The letter included detailed drawings in the style of Heath Robinson. Head Office considered it but the plans fell through. Boom Boom!

CRIME WATCH

Not long after the counter leap we experienced two further incidents. The first was the mysterious disappearance of one of the till bags. It was usual practice at the close of business for the cash from each till to be placed in a leather bag secured by a small padlock. These were then placed in the branch safe and locked away until the next day.

One morning Jean, our head cashier came into my office looking rather sheepish. "One of the till bags is missing" she declared somewhat anxiously. I immediately went to the safe to check but it was true, there were only five bags, not the usual six. She insisted that she had counted them all in but was clearly unable to count them all out. Feeling concerned we went back to the tills but there was nothing there. We searched everywhere, again and again without any luck. How could this have happened? Where was the bag?

I rang HO to report the problem and was told that someone from internal audit would drive over to take charge. In the meantime I was to inform the local police. A couple of hours later we had both the police and internal audit carrying out an investigation.

Our young trainee Neill appeared particularly worried, as he and his friend had returned to the branch after closing to have a bite to eat before going into town, but they were soon cleared and reassured. After much scratching of heads and speculation it was generally assumed that somehow the bag had been left out and removed by the cleaner's husband or son who had been covering for the cleaner that day. They both mysteriously disappeared for a while after the incident although nothing was ever proven. We reviewed our cashing up process and bag counting became a strict two-person discipline.

I don't seriously think there was any connection but a week later I received a phone call from the police one Saturday at about 10pm. The young officer reported that my office window had been smashed. I drove into town and was met by the policeman who asked me to check if anything was missing from my office. This seemed to be a strange request as there was no way anyone could have climbed through the window without cutting themselves to ribbons. Eventually he passed me the phone number of a 24hr glazier, shrugged and disappeared. I was left sitting at my desk in the dark listening to the pubs turning out at 11pm whilst waiting for the repairman. It was a strange experience hearing the 'witty' comments of passers-by as they viewed the damage. The best was not a comment but the tuneless refrain of three or four chaps singing, "I love the sound of breaking glass" the

Nick Lowe song that reached number 7 in 1978. The repairman made a great job of securely boarding it up and I returned to my bed around midnight.

ONWARDS AND UPWARDS.

One windy morning in November 1985 I received a call from my old boss, Mike Blades. He was now in charge of the entire branch network at HO and told me I that was to be appointed Regional Manager for the twenty branches in North Wales and Western region. No interview this time, just a straightforward promotion. I was thrilled! I immediately picked up the branch directory to check where the Regional Office was located. I was delighted to see it was in the lovely town of Chester. Sue was pleased for me, but sad that we would have to leave behind a number of good friends and the lovely village which we had made home.

AU REVOIR HULL

My leaving do was a memorable night at "Froggies, the fun place to eat!". Someone mentioned Froggies leggies and I was immediately challenged to put both of my legs behind my head. I duly obliged and have the photographs to prove it. I also stood on my chair and played the spoons, following my star turn with an impromptu dance routine with young Neill with me wearing Sally's flowing coat. A memorable night!

I had learnt a lot at Hull, mostly importantly how to select, manage and motivate a larger team. I had also started to see the bigger picture in financial services by becoming involved with housing issues both locally and nationally. My media experience had moved on from press to radio and television; and my marketing skills had been honed through numerous promotions. I enjoyed that my boss had left me alone to do my own thing. His only motivating words were when he addressed a regional meeting declaring "We need to get the SHIP back on the ROAD!" Dear Mike, bless him.

CHAPTER 7
NORTH WEST REGION
NOVEMBER 1985 TO DECEMBER 1988

When I rang John Carrier, the Regional Manager whom I was replacing, I was surprised and a little disappointed to learn that the branch directory I had consulted was out of date. The Chester location was only temporary and the office had moved to be above the new branch premises in Warrington.

THE TOWN

Warrington is situated on the banks of the River Mersey some twenty miles east of Liverpool and twenty miles west of Manchester. Although originally in Lancashire, it became part of Cheshire in 1974. The current population is estimated at over 200k, doubling in size since it was designated a "New Town" in 1968.

Close to the M62, M6 and M56 it is home to several distribution centres. The first Ikea store in the UK was opened just outside the town in 1987. Famous people born in Warrington include DJ Chris Evans and actor Sue Johnston. George Formby is buried there.

DAY ONE

The Regional office was situated on the top floor of a three-storey building, with the branch at ground level and Regional Surveyors office on the first floor. I pressed the intercom located at the rear of the premises, announced myself and heard a click as the back door unlocked. I was greeted at the top of the stairs by a man who confidently introduced himself as 'John'. He had short dark hair, glasses and a face with almost weasel like features. He introduced me to Lorna, his secretary. She was in her early twenties and had long brown hair. My friend Andy was later to describe her as having a passing resemblance to the actress Barbara Stanwyck. I was then introduced to Carolyn, the final member of the small team and Lorna's assistant.

I was immediately faced with making a significant decision, the first of many in my new role. Carolyn offered me a drink so as usual I politely requested coffee with milk and one sugar. Somewhat apologetically Carolyn informed me that they did not have any sugar as no one took it. She offered to nip out and get some but not wanting to appear awkward I said I could do without. That was the moment I gave up sugar in drinks and have never looked back!

THE BRIEFING

John took me into his office for a briefing. Somewhat like the man, the room appeared pretty characterless but functional. His organisational talents became apparent as he explained some of the systems he had introduced to enable smooth running of the twenty branch offices. There were two that seemed particularly effective: the letter reply deadline, and a comprehensive quarterly report. I liked them both but was looking forward to seeing how well they went down with the managers. It was clear John took his role seriously. I could count the number of times he smiled during the meeting on one finger, and that was only when Carolyn asked him if he too would like a cup of sugarless coffee.

Following a second slow slurp of coffee, John commenced to report at length a number of security concerns at Walton Vale branch. Situated in an inner city area of Liverpool close to Goodison Park, the home of Everton Football Club, the branch suffered more break-ins than any other in the region. The poor manager was being called out at all hours and the situation needed resolving.

On a lighter note John declared that Chester was the best performing branch for business development. The newly appointed manager, Ken Brown, was both very keen and capable. Ken's appointment had been made possible by moving the previous manager to semi-retirement at the much smaller Moreton branch located on the Wirral. John continued to sing Ken's praises. He concluded his appraisal by proclaiming that nothing was "beyond our Ken!". I noted the reference to the comedy radio sketch show from the 60's and laughed out loud, only to realise that John was yet again being entirely serious.

John provided me with a thorough profile of all twenty managers and key branch staff. I was impressed by his work even though his style appeared to be very different from my more relaxed and open approach. He had built a solid foundation from which I could enjoy developing managers with encouragement to flourish.

John set off to start his new role as one of three Operations Managers. He would be reporting to my old boss from the West Midlands, Mike Blades. I wasn't sure how they would get on, as John was clearly someone who liked to be in control. John was replacing Ian Lees who was leaving to work full time for a charity. I was given Ian's Ford Granada while waiting for my high spec Montego. I was never really interested in cars as this choice probably confirms.

OUT AND ABOUT

Within the first few days I did two things. I decided to visit as many of the twenty branches as possible and arranged to get all the managers together in the meeting room at Regional Office and outline my plans. The largest branches were at Chester, Liverpool and Ellesmere Port.

There was a familiar face at Chester where I found Mark Roden with whom I had worked briefly at Hull. The Manager, Ken, was a large chap who I instantly connected with. About a year younger than me he was very bright and could switch from very serious to very amusing in a flash. I sensed he was testing me at first to ensure he could make the switch, as this may not have been possible with my predecessor.

He told me he had something to show me outside. I thought Ken was going to ask me to admire the way the branch architecture fitted into the ancient city wall. But no, he asked me to read the window display of the three Marler Haley panels. They read; "the Leeds" …"the way to"…" laughing all." It should of course read; "Laughing all the way to the Leeds". Ken was laughing and so was I. Apparently David Gaskell was responsible for window displays. David had been at the branch for many years and had become part of the furniture. A well-meaning chap with a heart of gold. The customers loved him. He lived with his twin brother, and Ken and Mark were not sure if they occasionally swapped places. David readily admitted that when they were buying clothes, he would ask his brother to try a jacket on and if he liked what he saw he would say "I'll have it".

Ellesmere Port was about a twenty minutes' drive from Chester just off the M53. Manager Barry Walsh was ex-HO with a very friendly welcoming approach. His reputation for recruiting attractive staff was justified as soon as I entered. He had more than a passing resemblance to the actor David Jason or was it Del Boy from Only Fools and Horses. Barry was never too keen on the latter. He was older than me and was described by John as "a safe pair of hands", but I soon realised he still had more to offer.

To travel from Ellesmere Port to the centre of Liverpool takes about thirty minutes allowing for the tunnel. Alwyn Blackburn ran a well-organised branch in Lord Street. He was easily the oldest manager in the Region and not too far off retirement. Solid as a rock but perhaps a little set in his ways, which was not surprising. He gave me a handshake signalling one of his other interests. It wasn't long before he asked me if I was interested in joining the Masons but I decided not to mention my previous experience with similar male groups i.e. boozy joke telling (Round Table) and topless table tennis (Rotary). Alwyn was a gentleman and took my polite rejection well.

HELLO AND GOODBYE

During my re-location period I was booked into a very basic hotel, its only convenience being that it was about ten minutes' drive from the office. The rooms were so small I could touch both walls as I stretched out on the single bed. I had stayed in much better hotels when I was a mere trainee so felt I would be justified in seeking improvement. Two serendipitous events resolved my temporary discomfort.

At this time there were ten training managers each responsible for a couple of regions. My Region shared Andy Clark with the adjacent Greater Manchester Region. Andy and I had become friends when we were both trainees in the Midlands so I asked for his advice on where to live. He suggested that if we were prepared to live a little further out of town we would find some good value houses being built in Holmes Chapel.

At the earliest opportunity I was off down the M6 to junction 18. This was about twenty miles away from the office but as the journey was mostly motorway, it only took about forty minutes.

The new "executive" estate was being built by Beazer Homes and the plots were just being released. Sue and I loved the village location of Holmes Chapel. We settled on a four bed detached house with south facing rear garden set in a small cul-de-sac, an ideal family home. Our house in North Ferriby had sold quickly, so while we were waiting for our new house to be built Sue and our three little ones moved in with her Mum and Dad and I resigned myself to living in my tiny box room for the duration.

On my journey back to Warrington I noticed a really nice hotel between Holmes Chapel and Knutsford and stopped to take a look. The Cottons was a modern hotel with seemingly everything you could ask for. I asked to speak to the manager and we soon agreed a much reduced price as long as booked a month at a time. Deal done and hardly any more expensive than the prison cell back in Warrington.

Back at the office and still only a few days behind my desk, a knock came on the door. It was the Warrington Manager, Dan

Heaphy. Dan and I had started at the same time back in Birmingham in 1974. In fact we had responded to the very same advertisement in the Birmingham Evening Mail. We had been on the same induction and reps courses and had passed our exams to qualify at the same final sitting. While I had been in Bridgwater, Cannock and Hull, Dan had been Manager at Stretford and now Warrington.

He was his usual pleasant self and got straight to the point. He was resigning and it was all my fault! He said that he felt that he wasn't progressing in his career and had dropped too far behind some of his peers. This was highlighted by the fact that we had started together and I was now his boss. He told me he had been offered a very good job with a firm of brokers in Chester. It was well paid and wouldn't require him to uproot his family to follow future promotion. I was disappointed to lose him but appreciated his position and wished him all the best.

What happened next was amazing! Dan's replacement as Branch Manager was to be none other than my good friend Andy Bates. I had not been involved in the selection but was delighted by the result. I welcomed him to the North by setting him up with a good deal at The Cottons. I now had a friend and colleague to share midweek evenings. Our expense allowance did not stretch to the Cotton's restaurant but we enjoyed many of the lower priced eateries in the area.

Following our decision, Andy and his wife Terri also bought a new house in Holmes Chapel just at the end of our road. Things were going well.

MOTIVATING THE BOYS

Early in the New Year I held my first regional meeting at the offices in Warrington. My main message was that things would stay pretty much as John had left them with a couple of important changes. The quarterly reviews although not universally popular would stay, but I would re-evaluate the content and all managers were invited to send in their suggested improvements. The only condition was that the change needed to be explained and justified. I would then re-issue the revised forms ready for the next quarter.

The other main change was that I wanted branches to be focused on the areas of business that made a real difference, the obvious one being mortgages. I also wanted us to be winners, beating targets and other regions with all staff sharing in our success. Thankfully there was a positive reaction.

THE WILD WEST

As spring beckoned I took to the road to north Wales to visit our two most westerly branches. First stop was Colwyn Bay. The branch was ranked quite low with only three staff. I don't think I had quite got through the door before the manager Des Whittome told me that this meant he was not allocated a company car and felt this was unfair. I genuinely sympathised with his position and repeated what I had said when he had raised the same issue at the recent regional meeting. Basically there were two ways to solve this: either put on enough business to move up the grades; or continue to lobby HO to change the car policy in his favour. I felt the latter was the most likely winner in the long run.

This was my first trip into Wales and I was curious to know what Des considered to be the main issues created by crossing the border. Did staff need to be able to speak the local language? Des was by no means a local as he was from the south of England. Both the cashier typists were locals but neither of them were fluent Welsh speakers. I found this surprising but apparently it was not uncommon in the area and didn't seem to create a barrier with customers.

Des was a real character, always cheerful (unless you mentioned cars). His was a pretty unusual existence being situated on the coast with only the slightly larger Llandudno branch his nearest neighbour.

I enjoyed some fantastic sea views on the short drive to Llandudno. Whereas the branch at Colwyn Bay was a fairly modern building with a traditional shop frontage, Llandudno had a very strange appearance. It was probably an old bank built from brick and concrete with a sandy red finish. There was little space for the Leeds signage with the lettering squashed to a point where it was difficult to read. I was reminded of Bridgwater branch's almost anonymous position.

The Llandudno manager was another familiar face. Mike Perry had joined the Leeds as a trainee at Birmingham Temple Row not long before I left for Wolverhampton. Mike was older than the usual intake of trainees back then. His hair was receding, but his smile never did. He was as positive as they come and great company. Mike informed me that my predecessor's instruction was to add as many Agents to his branch as possible. I told him that this was not what I wanted him to do. Agents were rarely cost effective and I felt his time would be better served on more profitable areas, as I had indicated at the recent regional meeting. Looking relieved Mike readily agreed.

He was keen to show me around his area. It was quite large and therefore incorporated varied communities including the Isle of Anglesey. After crossing the Menai Strait Mike asked me if I would like to visit Rhosneigr where his family had a holiday home. I readily agreed, hiding my innate nosiness behind a veneer of professional curiosity. The house, aptly named 'Sea View' was right on the beach next to a slipway that in years past had been used to launch the lifeboat. Mike proudly showed me around the large rooms with fantastic views of the sea saying that it could accommodate at least sixteen people. He commented that it would make a great venue for a regional meeting but I was thinking differently.

Keen to improve the bonding between managers across the Region I had been planning a team-building weekend and decided this would be the ideal venue. On the long drive back to The Cottons later that day I gave the idea further thought and decided to press ahead.

BOYS AND THE SANDY STUFF

An invitation was sent from Regional Office inviting all Branch Managers and senior Assistant Managers to attend a "Regional Conference (social)" at Mike's place in Rhosneigr on Anglesey from 6th to 8th June 1986.

The invitation included a typo which I hadn't spotted recommending a guided tour of local "hostileries". The price was set at a very affordable £5 per night. Sports facilities were to be made available including water skiing and windsurfing. Golf and beach football were also promised.

ON THE BEACH

There was an excellent response with eleven Managers and one Assistant Manager confirming attendance. In addition, Mike's two cousins Jon and Steve would be there to help with the water sports, making a total of fifteen. The house could just about cope with the numbers although six unlucky late comers had to sleep in the 'Dorm" Fortunately there was no need for bed sharing on this occasion. For the sake of completeness: the register was as follows:

Two nights:

Me
Andy Bates (Warrington)
Mike Perry (Llandudno)
Peter Maskrey (Crewe)
David Owen (Birkenhead)
Roger Sunderland (Wallasey)
Mark Roden (ABM Chester)

One night:

Ken Brown (Chester)
Jim Tomczyk (Maghull)
Terry Matthews (Wilmslow)
Liam Gallagher (not that one, Macclesfield)

Andrew Smith (Widnes)
John Andrews (Moreton)

My friend and Warrington Manager Andy accompanied me as
we left on Friday afternoon determined to get across to
Anglesey early and bag the best rooms. As we turned into the
parking area outside Sea View the sun dazzled across the
calm sea. It was a beautiful evening. Our eyes soon refocused
on the very impressive speedboat that Mike Perry's cousins
had brought across from Birmingham. Mike showed us around
the 3-story property and we chose two rooms with fantastic
views across the beach and out to sea. The rest of the guys
gradually arrived and the large kitchen soon became the focal
point. A late boozy night followed a welcome meal in the local
bistro.

One of the managers, Peter Maskrey (Crewe), had trained in
catering immediately after leaving school and much to our
delight produced a truly excellent cooked breakfast on our first
morning. The weather had turned but there were still those
who were desperate to test the water sports. Their numerous
attempts to stand up on skis against a lively sea were most
amusing for the watchers. After a pub lunch and a quick
snooze it was time for our own World Cup. In Mexico, England
had already lost to Portugal and drawn with Morocco and were
due to play their final qualifying game on the following
Wednesday.

We took to the beach and had just enough players to make
five per side. The two captains easily selected their
goalkeepers. As a youth Ken Brown had been on the books of
Dunfermline FC, as a keeper and David Owen (Birkenhead)
proved to be a natural in between the sticks (actually beach
cricket stumps). His nickname "The Cat" was an obvious
choice.

There were a couple of very skilful players notably Jim
Tomczyk (Maghull). The tough tackling Peter Maskrey ran
non-stop and kicked anything that moved, and plenty that
didn't move! The player that really stood out was Roger

Sunderland (Wallasey). Roger drifted so far out on his wing that it looked as though he was in the sea. At one point I was convinced he had lit a cigarette but couldn't be sure. The sand sapped our energy and we soon retired to the welcoming kitchen. This was just a few yards away for most of us, but quite a trek for the hapless Roger.

The evening was spent at the Plas Club, deemed to be the best 'club' in Rhosneigr. This could only have been because it was the ONLY club there. It was a very old-fashioned venue, more of a members' bar i.e. no music just food and drink. It was very dated but the meal and beer were adequate. Mike and his cousins were well known there and stayed on drinking, a decision which Mike regretted the next morning.

On our second morning we awoke to constant rainfall that looked set in for the day. Only the very keen golfers set off to tackle the Rhosneigr course dominated by the numerous sheep that patrolled virtually every hole with bruises providing evidence of errant ball striking. Playing conditions were further affected by the almost constant noise from the adjacent RAF base. There were low flying jets screaming over head or the whirling from the Sea King rescue helicopters.

The weekend was enjoyed by all and declared a success in terms of the team building. So much so that it was decided to book a return visit the following year extending it to include the whole of the Friday. Over thirty years later a dozen or so of us still meet up in Rhosneigr each May. Regulars from the original group include Mike P, Andy B, David O, and occasionally Jim T. Others have joined us over the years such as Barry Walsh (Ellesmere Port and Chester), Stuart Fearns (Liverpool and Warrington), John Moseley (Wallasey), Alan Todd (Prescot) and Andy Bullough (Chester, Ellesmere Port).

HOME IN HOLMES CHAPEL

Within a few days of returning from Rhosneigr the removal van was being unloaded outside our brand new house in Holmes Chapel. Whilst waiting patiently for the building work to be completed Sue and our three children had camped at her parent's house in Solihull for six months. It hadn't been easy, not least because Sue had suffered the loss of her dad Tom following what we thought was routine surgery.

One of the advantages of moving into a newly built property was that everyone in the Close was in the same position. Our friends Andy and Terri were just a few doors away, and we soon made friends with our new neighbours particularly Pam and Rick with whom we are still close today. The first time Andy and I spotted Pam as she was sunbathing on her front lawn. We instantly knew she and Rick were our kind of people!

FOOTBALL CRAZY

As winter approached, I learnt that Chester branch had a very good business relationship with the house builders Redrow. The founder and owner of Redrow was Steve Morgan, a passionate Liverpool FC fan. He regularly invited business contacts to a match at Anfield, which included a very pleasant lunch in the trophy room. Our Chester Manager Ken Brown had been invited to a match and asked me to join him.

I arrived quite early and made my way to the function suite. To my surprise I discovered it was almost empty. I noticed a man on his own stationed at the bar holding his glass tightly. I walked over and after being served I decided to make conversation. It was immediately apparent that English was not his first language, or maybe even his second. He was French, a fact that led to a slight feeling of panic as I recalled my French teacher's comment on my school report "Paul is cheerfully incompetent". Frenchie and I struggled on and I eventually discovered he was working as a pundit for a French television company. Thankfully Ken arrived to rescue me and we said 'au revoir'. With a smirk on his face Ken revealed that my new friend was Michel Platini the former French captain who had just retired from Juventus. Ooh la la! I had just been "chatting" with the French player of the century in total ignorance!

I was not the only one to make such a schoolboy error that day. On arrival Ken had smugly parked in what seemed to be a free zone with plenty of space. As he returned to his car after the match he began to realise why no one had parked there. Unfortunately, it turned out to be a police control area meaning Ken's car was now surrounded by police vehicles, including a caravan. A nice big sticker enclosing a fine was attached to his windscreen.

REGIONAL MEETING WITH LASTING EFFECTS

As the New Year began I decided it was time for another get together for the Region's managers. I liked to invite a guest speaker and this time Mark Waterhouse from Business Operations at HO came along to give us a "state of the nation" address, outlining the Society's performance and plans for the future. As usual we provided a buffet lunch using our regular outside caterer. These were the days when lunchtime wine was still provided although our offer of cheap Liebfraumilch was not appreciated by several of the budding wine buffs amongst us, notably Andy, (who still reminds me of my poor selection).

The meeting went well and Mark set off to make another presentation further south. The following morning the phones were red hot with managers across the Region reporting in sick. It soon became apparent that almost everyone who had attended the meeting was suffering from food poisoning. There was no alternative; I had to report the problem. There was a swift response from the authorities as they swooped on the caterer's premises. It turned out that she worked from her home. No bugs were discovered but her food hygiene processes were deemed not to comply with the current regulations and she was forced to cease trading immediately. I felt a stab of remorse but felt responsibility for my managers' health was greater. We tracked Mark down and luckily like me, he was fine. I think we had been protected by the cheap plonk!

PAY ATTENTION TO BUSINESS

Things were going well on the business front with our Region ahead of target and looking strong in comparison with the other regions. My boss, Roger Gray was both supportive and encouraging. It had identified that a key area for business growth was insurance, so a number of Regional Insurance Managers were duly appointed.

Our man was Steve Shakeshaft, affectionately known as "Shaky". There was nothing shaky about Steve. He was always immaculately dressed. So concerned was he about his appearance that he clipped a clothes peg on his car seat belt to protect his jacket and shirt from creasing. He was very eager to increase business and was soon seen by our managers as keen to help them. So much so that when it came to the frequent compulsory tests on their insurance knowledge, he was sure to add a nod or a wink to help his audience understand the importance of attending to key topics.

The area that most if not all Regions struggled with at that time was pension sales. HO arranged for three companies to hold seminars for every Region to help with understanding and sales. I decided to give my support by attending one or two. I have to admit I found the subject as dry as a desert. I sat quietly a few rows from the front as the chap from Prolific Insurance did his best to enthuse his audience. But after lunch and probably too much Liebfraumilch a number of heads began to droop. Suddenly the guest speaker pointed at Andrew Smith (Widnes) sitting in the front row and shouted, "He's asleep!" at which point poor Andrew shot bolt upright and was greeted by much laughter. I think everyone was just relieved that it hadn't been them caught nodding off. Andrew apologised and order was restored. Pension sales remained difficult but unshakeable Shaky relentlessly pressed forward.

CRIME WAVE

We were still suffering frequent attempts to break into Walton

Vale branch now managed by Mark Roach. They were always at night and fortunately there were no attempts to actually rob the branch during the day, much to the relief of the staff. A common joke running amongst the staff was that the prison around the corner was letting several of the inmates out at night to practice their trade. This 'practice' wasn't working though as the most they got away with was the £5 notes we kept in each drawer that set off the cameras when removed from their clips. As the thefts were at night the cameras were pretty useless in the dark so we failed to catch the culprits.

HO had introduced American Express Travellers Cheques at all branches. We kept very little cash in our safes overnight but the travellers cheques quickly mounted up. This soon became common knowledge amongst the criminal community and things started to happen.

The thieves were clever and did not try to rob the branch during working hours as this was riskier and carried a severe sentence, particularly if weapons were involved. Their tactic was to break into a branch in the early hours via the back door, remove the relatively small safe, and flee the scene in an unmarked van. The contents of the safe could then be removed at leisure.

Branch security was almost none existent. Neither the safe nor the back door were alarmed. Robberies continued particularly in the North West and the police seemed to suspect a particular family and began staking out selected branches and planting portable alarms. This tactic eventually worked, well to a degree. One of the police alarms went off and the Panda car was soon chasing a white van along the M6. The van swerved from side to side but the police car stuck firmly behind. Without warning the rear doors to the van were flung open. The police car made the mistake of closing in for a better view. This they got, but what they witnessed was a grey safe bouncing on the carriageway towards them. It distracted them from their view of the van. The police car ground to a halt. The chase was off but the safe was recovered. Arrests followed and things settled down. Security in the branches did improve after that but it took a while.

A different type of robbery happened in the neighbouring Greater Manchester Region. The manager of one of the city centre branches received a phone call CLAIMING TO BE from the Surveyors' department at Leeds HO. The caller said that they were closing in on an excellent property purchase in the area but they had to pay the deposit in cash the next day or the deal would be lost. He was instructed to arrange for several thousand pounds in cash to be in the branch early the next morning. Someone from HO would be at the back door at 8am to collect the funds. Next morning the cash was handed over (amazingly without identity checks or signatures) and never seen again.

"NEVER!" I hear you cry. Yes never, we woz 'ad and the money was lost. The Manager claimed that he had been framed. The incident was thoroughly investigated but after a while the hunt ended, as did someone's career.

OH WHAT A CIRCUS

It was that time again when in the middle of winter managers met up in Leeds. The Annual General Meeting had for many years taken place at Leeds Town Hall but it was not available so the AGM took place at the Grand Theatre located on New Briggate.

The Directors shuffled in and took their seats on the stage. The great and the good looked comfortable and ready to go through the formalities, thoroughly prepared for any difficult questions from the floor. What they couldn't see above them was a banner left from the previous night's entertainment proclaiming *Colonel Crackers Crazy Circus Has Come To Town!*

The tittering rose and fell much to the bemusement of the Directors. Eventually we settled down and as usual all the votes went as expected and we all rushed down to the Queens Hotel for the free bar. Poor Howard Briggs, the

Society's secretary was left alone to explain the banner to the somewhat puzzled Directors.

Back at The Queens, hundreds of managers sat for dinner. This year there was an added extra, a new award called the Enterprise Trophy. It was to be presented to the branch demonstrating the most outstanding performance. Not just business results but other initiatives such as press articles and community involvement. I had nominated Chester branch and Ken and his team had made the short list. Their results were so strong I was confident they would win. The lights dimmed, the drums rolled and I gasped as Chester were announced beaten in to second place by Chris Kelly's King Edward St team. Ken and I were gutted but the smiles soon returned to our faces when the Society's solicitor, Ann O'Brien, gave a superb speech mimicking Margaret Thatcher. It brought the house down.

WAPPING DOCK

In addition to Redrow, we had a very good working relationship with the country's largest builder, Barratt Homes. In 1982 they built over 16,000 new homes using controversial timber frames and offering white goods as incentives. By the late 80's they were changing their approach and trying to move upmarket. They were also known for their TV adverts featuring the actor Patrick Allen leaping in and out of the Barratt helicopter. He was known for many TV roles and also for narrating the first Blackadder series.

In the spring of 1988 I was approached by Barratt's Regional Sales Manager and asked to consider an interesting proposal. They had bought an old warehouse in the run-down area known as Wapping Dock in Liverpool's dock land area. They planned to turn the warehouse into spacious apartments. One or two lenders had been cool to initial approaches and they were looking for a lender to take a positive view of the development. Barratt explained that if we considered the units to be suitable mortgage security we would be in prime position for mortgage referrals.

Our Surveyor Manager, John Sharman was an experienced valuer and former estate agent. He knew the area well and was happy to view the proposal. We met the Barratt people at the docks and were escorted around the empty warehouse. After viewing the various plans and artists impressions, John and I agreed that we liked the layout and security of the apartments. Our only real concern was the surrounding area. The docks were in a poor state, although the proposed apartment prices seemed to reflect this. Barratt were keen to regenerate the whole area and planned to move along the waterfront with further developments if this one proved successful.

It did. In fact the sales were so good that we had to stop accepting mortgage applications as we had set a maximum share to avoid over exposure. Barratt soon successfully developed a second warehouse on the docks. These units weren't as spacious as those at Wapping but still sold well enough.

The success of this project led to a strong business relationship with Barratt that was of benefit to both parties.

BIG CHANGES

On the wider business front there was excitement across the whole of the business when it was announced that Mike Blackburn was joining the Leeds as Chief Executive. Mike had been at Lloyds Bank for more than twenty years and was currently CEO at Access, their credit card subsidiary. In his mid-40's, Mike was a strongly built chap with an imposing stance yet pleasant approach. To some he resembled Desperate Dan from the Dandy comic without the stubble or cowboy boots! He was the first outside leader the Society had ever appointed. Excitement grew as the prospect of significant change loomed.

However changes came slowly at first. He brought one person with him from Lloyds, Norman Thompson. He was a very capable public relations man. Slowly but surely Mike replaced other key management and director positions bringing in Chris Chadwick as Commercial Director from Next, and Judy Atchison as Head of Group Marketing from RHM (Rank Hovis McDougall). This was just the beginning.

To the outside world, evidence of things changing would have first become apparent with the appointment of Abbot Mead Vickers as our advertising agents shortly before Mike joined. The now famous Liquid Gold adverts, featuring George Cole, hit our TV screens in September 1985. The advertising regulations prevented him from being overtly featured as Arthur Daley from Minder, but the portrayal was unmistakably 'Arthur'. The campaign had huge impact and it was estimated that around 95% of the UK population became aware of 'Liquid Gold' as a result.

A DIVIDED COUNTRY

In the middle of August I received a very interesting call from my boss Roger Gray. He told me that our new CEO had brought in a team of management consultants to help formulate the Society's business strategy. He asked me to come over to HO to work on plans for developing the branch network.

When I arrived in Leeds, Roger led me to Mike Blades' office. My old boss was on his usual August break, but now on his desk were a series of maps covering the whole of the UK. Roger explained that consideration was being given to a move to fewer, larger "Areas" as opposed to more than twenty Regions. My task was to divide the country into areas of similar business weight and numbers of branches. I also had to propose where the area administration hubs should be centred.

Over the next few days I had a lot of fun drawing rings on maps and eventually settled on eight key areas, which had virtually picked themselves: Scotland (plus a bit of the North East); North West (maybe a bit of bias here); Yorkshire (due to home strength); plus four equal weight areas in the Midlands

South East, South West, and London. As I studied the maps I couldn't help wondering where I would end up if this change came to fruition.

THE CULL

The night of the long knives came about on the last day of the financial year, 30th September. More than one general manager was "released from their duties'. Ted Germaine took the news particularly badly. Ted was popular in many quarters but was said to be prone to making some very strange decisions that many of his colleagues found hard to understand and often difficult to implement. At first, he didn't seem to accept that he had been 'released' although when a member of Ian Goodwin's pension team tried to ring Ted with his pension quotes he allegedly answered his phone saying, "Ted here, I'm a bit tied up at the moment so can't take your call, but I love being tied up!". He was a character but it was sad to see him become very bitter as he dragged out his departure.

PRESSING ALL THE WRONG BUTTONS

I didn't have to wait long to see how I would be affected. All Regional Managers, plus a number of those thought to be close to that level, were summoned to attend a day long assessment centre at Saville and Holdsworth's offices in the centre of London. Some of the older existing Regional Managers were particularly worried, as they knew that there were only going to be eight Heads Of Field Operations (HOFOs) and eight Area Sales Manager (ASM) positions. It was generally assumed that the ASM positions would not be deemed suitable for older more traditional Regional Managers and it turned out to be true.

We were really put through our paces that day with a range of individual tests and group exercises. It was so stressful that half way through the morning one of our group shot into the loo and was heard to be calling for help from "Hughie". I thought I was doing ok, until at the end of the psychometric assessment I inadvertently closed the computer and wiped the whole test. I was reassured that I could retake the test at lunchtime but this meant I was left with no time to have a stroll or clear my head ready for the afternoon sessions. That night as I sat on the train home I remember my head pounding from the relentless concentration and wondering what the future would hold.

A FEW SHOCKS

I didn't have long to wait before I found out that I had been appointed HOFO for the North West. I could not have been happier. Promotion, no house move and knowledge of a third of the new Area made the change almost perfect. Equally good news was that my ASM would be David "spill the beans" George who I knew well from my time in the Midlands. Of the eight HOFO's, five were current Regional Managers, the other three being my current boss Roger (Yorkshire) and his fellow Operations Manager Stuart Morris (South East). It wasn't good news for everyone though. Most surprisingly, my old boss Mike Blades had been appointed HOFO for the Eastern area, a clear demotion. I did not see this coming even though he appeared to have been sidelined during the restructuring as evidenced by my mapping exercise in his office.

There were a few raised eyebrows following Arthur Haycock's promotion to HOFO for the South West as he was considered by some to be a bit "old school" Apparently, he had achieved the top score at the assessment centre which could not be ignored.

The new North West Area had sixty-three branches in contrast to the twenty I was looking after. These included eight branches in Northern Ireland. In addition to having a new ASM, my area office would have four other managers looking after personnel, training, insurance and surveying. A new suite of offices would be needed. There was much to do.

THE BALLOON GOES UP

Amongst all the excitement was some sad news. My good friend Andy had decided to leave the Leeds. During the re-shuffle he had been offered a job with the Norwich and Peterborough Building Society managing several local branches. Andy's new role meant a move back to Norfolk, near to where his wife Terri came from and her parents still lived. I was happy for him but felt sad to be losing both a true friend and a very capable manager who I was sure would progress further had he stayed. All I could do was wish him well and promise to stay in touch.

He had a memorable leaving do at a Warrington pub where the highlight was the appearance of a scantily dressed young woman strategically covered in balloons. Andy's task was to burst each balloon. He performed this with great precision leaving the young lady to exit in a hurry. Well it made a change from a stripping policewoman.

UP ANOTHER NOTCH

I had enjoyed the role of Regional Manager particularly learning how to manage from a distance. I also enjoyed helping people develop and seeing them promoted. I was both excited and a little nervous at the prospect of the next step, which at that stage seemed to be more of a huge leap.

CHAPTER 8
HEAD OF FIELD OPERATIONS NORTH WEST
JANUARY 1989 TO JUNE 1991

David and I had lots to do. We needed to amalgamate three different regions into one cohesive Area, appoint new staff and find new premises. All of this whilst deciding how we were going to run things between us. At least I didn't have to move the family this time, or did I?

DIVIDING UP AGAIN

David was a pleasure to work with. He was thoughtful, diligent and intelligent. He was not afraid to express his opinions, but this was always done with a good sense of humour – a real bonus when working with me. There was however, one major drawback, he was a Stoke City FC supporter.

We divided responsibility for the branches between us with David as ASM getting the lion's share enabling me to concentrate on other areas. I decided David should take on all of the eight branches in Northern Ireland. I reasoned that being a separate country with its own practices, particularly employment law, it made business sense for just one of us to tackle this and it might as well be David. Besides it would be more cost effective with fewer flights and overnight stays required.

Our first task was to show our faces to all our staff as soon as possible so together we set off on a whistle stop tour. This was a great opportunity to talk to David at length and to develop our thoughts on managing an Area that had many newly delegated powers. Most of the visits went well, apart from our trip to Blackpool. The manager was John Cotterell an ex-member of Business Operations at HO. Blackpool had two branches with John managing the much larger office in the centre of the town. I couldn't immediately put my finger on it but during our visit I sensed there was something not quite right. This feeling was compounded when after leaving the branch we retreated to the hotel that John had booked for us. This was out of season Blackpool so the choice of accommodation must have been extensive. However, John had made an interesting decision to place his two new bosses in a fleapit. To say it was a dump would be unfair, it was far worse than that! This was not a good start.

The rest of our tour was very rewarding. We met some great staff with positive attitudes at almost every one of the sixty-three branches.

PREMISES PREMISES

David and I had a pretty good idea of the sort of premises we needed for our Area offices and with the help of HO Property Services / Surveyors it wasn't long before we found what we were looking for. Stuart Smith from HO quickly pointed us in the direction of a development on the edge of town backing on to the Rugby League ground at Wilderspool. St James Business Centre offered a number of offices of various sizes. There was plenty of free parking and even good restaurant facilities. We snapped up a first floor suite and were soon working with John Pickering, a very helpful young chap from property services to shape our new domain.

IN THE PINK

Our new home was completely empty which meant we had plenty of space to play with to provide individual offices, a large meeting room and an open administration area. John was great and soon came up with a suitable design.

I said a fond goodbye to black holes and cupboard offices and gave a welcome hello to a large office that could also be used as a meeting room. Was I posing? No, just being practical. The overriding colour scheme for the whole office was pink. Yes pink. Sounds a bit odd but we thought it looked classy. The offices needed to be constructed before we could move in but were soon ready to function.

BAD NEWS

In addition to David and I, the new management team consisted of Area Insurance Manager (AIM) Steve Shakeshaft, and Area Training Manager (ATM) Phil Moss. The major change for them was that they both now reported to me rather than HO and had a much wider brief. In addition I was now responsible for personnel and needed to recruit an experienced HR manager.

After one very good candidate withdrew John Holmes in HO Personnel came to the rescue and put us in touch with someone he and his wife Mary knew. We quickly appointed Alison Leftley and were back on track.

CAPTAIN BOB

My new boss was Bob Humphreys. He had previously been Assistant General manager IT at HO and had been fully involved with the restructuring, working closely with the management consultants brought in by CEO Mike Blackburn.

Bob was positive, energetic and keen for the new Area teams to meet up. David and I, together with our wives (both called Sue) were invited with managers from the other seven Areas to a two-day meeting at the Chevin Lodge Hotel near Leeds.

As we arrived the snow was gently falling adding a fairy-tale element to the attractive timber lodges. They were a little chilly but Bob and his wife Sheila hosted a great welcome meal.

It was good to meet up with all the other HOFOs, ASMs and their wives. Bob chaired a business meeting highlighting his thoughts on how we would operate and inviting other HO managers to share their plans.

That night we all boarded a coach to take us for a meal at the posh Pool Court where CEO Mike and his wife Louise hosted a very pleasant evening. I realised how fortunate I was to be part of this new team.

NEW TOYS

Along with our new roles came an increase in the car allowance. David and I both chose Vauxhall Carltons. Not only did we get shiny new cars, we also received our first car phones. These were hard wired into the car for calls only. They were nothing like today's smartphones but we were delighted. The excitement soon wore off but they proved to be essential equipment in our new world. It was rumoured that one senior manager being unfamiliar with such mod-cons had tried to converse through the air vent. As his frustration grew so did the hot air in both directions.

MOVING THE FAMILY

Back in Holmes Chapel our next-door neighbours had put their house up for sale. It was quite a bit larger than ours with two extra rooms on the ground floor and was situated in a significantly bigger plot. As the family were growing up and we all needed more space we decided to go for it. We quickly sold our house to a lovely Scottish family and arranged for their removal firm to move us next door at an amazingly good price.

It turned out to be a very wise move as shortly after our move Sue's mum suffered a heart attack and moved in with us for a 'short stay' that lasted twelve happy years.

WHO SELLS WINS

As the new team began to settle David came up with a great idea to improve sales by putting together a sales training team. Three very capable trainers were transferred from their branches: Denise Clark and Cheryl Turley were skilfully led by Grace Ruleman.

Their task was to help train branch staff to professionally sell Leeds' products. They were a great team and the concept worked extremely well. Very soon David was presenting "Who

Sells Wins" awards each month.

Using sales targets was a prevalent motivator at the time, sometimes leading to an overzealous approach. This was an attempt to try to make sure that customers were sold suitable products. There is no doubt that it improved the knowledge of our staff and their confidence to approach customers correctly.

SUPER TROOPERS

The ability to make our own decisions also led to the introduction of Area Supernumeraries. They were managed by Area Office and were sent to help out at offices that were short staffed, often due to illness. The first two appointments were Sue Randles and Fran Hurst, both experienced and capable cashier typists who could fit in anywhere.

They were also useful in their ability to assess staff 'temperature' throughout the Area. It was a delicate task asking them to report back any interesting observations without them being seen as Area spies. Sue and Fran turned out to be excellent additions to the Area team, they were universally liked and frequently welcomed by branches under pressure.

I was very lucky to still have Lorna Baddeley as my PA. She was very good at her job, well respected and knew at least a third of all our Area staff, having been with me at Regional Office. David appointed Debbie Carter as his PA. Debbie had been PA to the Manchester Regional manager Norman Lowry, which meant she had excellent knowledge of another third of the staff. Bringing their exceptional people skills and knowledge to the role, Lorna and Debbie were a tremendous asset to us.

The staff numbers in the office continued to grow as Sue Marrow (Phil's Training PA) and Angela Booth (Alison's Personnel PA) joined. We also brought in two Gails - Roberts and Andrews as office juniors. I frequently got the two Gails mixed up even though they were very different: one was quite reserved and the other wasn't. They were both lovely young girls who soon became an important part of the team.

ISLAND IN THE SUN

We had been very busy following the launch of the new Area, and much had changed although one important event remained sacred – the Rhosneigr weekend. The date was set for our third visit. Most of the previous attendees turned up, and there were several new faces too.

One of the new crew was John Moseley the new manager at Wallasey. Ex-Wallasey manager Roger Sunderland had been strangely drawn to the sea on a past visit to Rhosneigr so the natural question was whether John would 'paddle' in his footsteps.

I will let John tell the story himself:

"I had some experience of sailing but absolutely none of windsurfing. However, after half an hour's instruction from Mike Perry and still in those days being young enough to believe myself bullet proof, with borrowed wetsuit I set out on what was even then, quite an old and heavy windsurfer. Lack of experience showed in that I was fine going in a straight line, but turning, which involves the delicate manoeuvre of tipping the mast forward and stepping round it to the other side of the board at precisely the right moment was a trickier skill to master and so usually resulted in me falling off and ignominiously remounting.

After a couple of hours of long tacks followed by sudden disembarkments at each turn I decided I was quite a long way out and it was time to head back to shore. Just as I was congratulating myself on a successful turn the mast suddenly disconnected from the board, one of the stainless steel split-pins had fallen out. It rolled tantalisingly across the board as I made a desperate lunge to grab it. I succeeded only in falling off the board and watching as the pin fell through the astonishingly clear water and into Davy Jones locker, where it remains to this day.

Now, part of Mike's half hour instruction had been about how to do a self-rescue. This involves rolling the sail around the mast, placing it lengthways on the board, laying on top of it and paddling with one's arms. Now remember that I was quite a long way from the shore at this point, so resigned to a long paddle I make a start for home. After half an hour of paddling I was beginning to feel a bit tired and so stopped and stood up on the board to see how much further there was to go. It's at this point that I was shocked to discover that the tide had taken me about twice as far out as I was when I started paddling. The beach had receded to a thin yellow line and the people on it to no more than pin-pricks. I don't know if you have ever experienced that knotted feeling in the pit of your stomach or the pins and needles as the blood drains from your body into your limbs and you think to yourself "I might die here" but I certainly have.

Fortunately, but unknown to me, at this moment, David Owen then manager at Birkenhead, a sailor of some considerable experience, realised that he hadn't seen the sail come out of the water for some time. So, he walked down to the waterfront and asked a guy on a jet ski to go out and check my position. Rescue duly arrived in the shape of a jet ski. We took some ropes from the sail and used them to make a towrope for the stricken windsurfer and I was towed to safety. I explained later that being towed by a jet ski is not the most comfortable experience. When you breathe it's a bit of a toss-up as to whether you get a lungful of air or a lungful of water, but at the time my gratitude was such that it seemed unreasonable to complain."

NOW A VIEW FROM THE BEACH

It was a beautiful sunny day, probably one the best we have ever had when John set off for his first attempt at windsurfing. A group of us sat comfortably on deck chairs, beers in hand and a clear view across the beach to a calm sea.

We soon fell into our usual routine of sipping cool beers and moving our conversation from the topically flippant - current price of beer, to the topically thought provoking - the impact of AIDS and the government's warning; "Don't die of ignorance".

After quite some time I noticed that John was far out to sea but he was obviously enjoying himself as he was waving to us. Mike Perry jokingly recalled the old coast guard advert from the late sixties: "Look Petunia he's waving to us". Oh how we chuckled as we reached for another beer! However as time went on, and the beer stocks became low, we thought again about John. By now he looked as though he was bound for Ireland and we started to become concerned. David Owen set off down the beach to ask one of the many jet skiers enjoying the lovely weather if they could go to check him out. To everyone's relief he was rescued and returned safely to the shore. John trudged towards looking exhausted but very relieved.

ANOTHER CLOSE SHAVE

One dice with death in a day turned out not to be enough for John. Later that evening about fifteen of us went to a local restaurant for dinner after which we planned to join the locals in the pub for a "lock in". On the way there, we noticed a gang of the local "youf" eyeballing us, but they left us alone. We didn't all leave the restaurant together and on arrival at the pub we realised that the group had become separated. John, ever the team player, volunteered to go back to the restaurant to tell the others where we were but unfortunately by the time he arrived they had already left so he started walking back towards the pub hoping to spot them. He didn't find any of our group, but what he did find were the aforementioned local "youf". This time, spotting a lone 'outsider' they started to follow him, slow hand clapping and chanting in Welsh. Now it could have been that they were wishing him "Good evening and welcome to Wales" but it sounded more like "We are going to beat the s**t out of you, you English B*****d!"
 Understandably John started walking faster, and then faster. By the time he made the pub door, now locked of course, (because that's the point of a "lock in"), he was sprinting fit to give Mo Farrah, quite literally, a run for his money. Fortunately for John, Mike Perry an even bigger team player had taken it on himself to look out for John and was stood by the door ready to let him in, just in the nick of time. John never was able to work out whether it was the luckiest day or unluckiest day of his life.

GOLF OF COURSE

Golf was now firmly established as part of the Rhosneigr weekend. I'm not great at golf but consider myself to be reasonably capable and always gave my best. I could, however, pride myself on being pretty proficient at maths. That year I excelled myself.

There were eight of us set to play the sheep infested Rhosneigr course. As we stood on the first tee I suggested the teams would fall neatly into two 2's and a 4. The laughter was instant before it was suggested to me that two teams of four might by more suitable.

I was given the nod to make the first drive from the elevated first tee. Immediately in front of me but set down below, was a trailer being used by a member of the green staff who was standing well out of range. It was well below the tee and therefore not obstructing play. I struck my golf ball firmly but it sailed low, into the side of the trailer and came straight back at me. I ducked and turned to watch it land some yards behind the tee. The 140 yard par 3 was now 170 yards. I joined in the laughter and proceeded to continue with yet another unimpressive round of golf.

This third year set the scene for many future successful gatherings. The Rhosneigr weekend is still held each May all these years later.

BREAKFAST AT ST JAMES'S

Back in Warrington I now had a large team to manage, which meant good communication was an essential component of my job. I introduced breakfast meetings for the whole team at 8.30am every other Monday in the ground floor restaurant. These meetings proved to be popular, as did the excellent breakfasts we enjoyed. It was a relaxed format where information flowed freely.

There was one particularly memorable breakfast held on the 2nd April 1990 when the whole of our heavily laden breakfast table shook and clattered violently. At first we thought there had been a collision outside, but later discovered we had in fact experienced an earthquake measuring 5.1 on the Richter scale. Even Shaky was shaken.

TRAINEES STILL NEEDED

Despite the slowdown in branch openings we still needed to have a good flow of management trainees. Peter Maskrey had a good reputation for developing trainees and when he was manager at Crewe had taken on a young lad called David Hughes.

When he interviewed for a management trainee Peter always threw in a topical question to start a discussion to help the candidate relax and get them talking. It also showed their awareness of current affairs, and perhaps if they read a quality newspaper. He liked to see if they had opinions on various matters and could express those opinions clearly. Peter wasn't really bothered what their opinion was and would tell them that, it was the discussion that mattered.

When Peter interviewed David Hughes the issue of the day was Cruise Missiles being held on an American airbase in this Country. It had led to protesters flocking to the camp at Greenham Common.

The time came in the interview for Peter's usual topical question; "What do you think about Cruise Missiles?" Young David looked puzzled, stroked his chin, pondered thoughtfully for quite a number of seconds and then said, "I didn't know Crewe had any missiles"

Peter laughed, as that was possibly the only answer he hadn't considered! Not surprisingly David was given the job. Thankfully he turned out to have a good career with the Leeds.

DOWN THE DRAIN

Training Manager Phil Moss was renowned for providing good support for the trainees. He ran a series of workshops to help them prepare for their assessment interview at HO. Passing this enabled promotion to the next level.

I would often pop in to the workshops to offer encouragement, as well as to get a feel for the progress individual trainees were making. An important topic for trainees was understanding the corporate structure, including knowledge of the Board of Directors. At one session I was sitting quietly in the corner when Phil asked an MT to reel off the names of the non-executive directors, one of whom was called Geoffrey Armitage. The young trainee successfully rattled off several names and then stumbled slightly as he tried to recall the next. He smiled with relief and confidently offered "Armitage Shanks!". It was clear that the other trainees were desperate to take the p**s following the reference to the sanitary company but only laughter surfaced.

GIRLS ALLOWED

We had recruited our first female trainees a couple of years previously and now we had our first two female Managers. Jane Blackwell came through after working at Walton Vale and Warrington. A very capable and enthusiastic MT. Jane was not afraid to speak her mind even if doing so resulted in her turning bright red. Jane was appointed to Maghull just north of Liverpool.

Coincidentally the other new Manager was also called Jane. Jane Waring had progressed well during a spell at St Helens and was appointed to manage Crosby branch located near the docks in Liverpool. Jane soon settled in and made a few changes, including reviewing the office utilities. She was really pleased to tell me that she had saved money by cancelling the standing charge for gas, as this was not needed. She wasn't quite so pleased when the office became increasingly colder as winter approached. Neither were her staff.

The two Janes were the first of many female Managers and were seen as trail blazers by those that followed their successful path.

HOME ARRANGER

Since his arrival CEO Mike Blackburn had been exploring ways to develop a clear identity for The Leeds. We wanted to stand out from the other 400 or so societies and take on the banks. The outcome of research and much hard work was the "Vision" focusing on the home.

Branches were to be reconfigured to subtly resemble the home. Each branch would have a dedicated member of staff covering all aspects of the home buying process and take much of the stress out of the move. The Home Arranger was born.

This was to take a while to develop and fortunately our Burnley branch was chosen as a test site. Manager Bill Haworth and our first Home Arranger Sarah Coupe responded excitedly to the challenge. The concept was to make house buying a much easier, simpler and stress-free process by handing over all the work, other than the legal necessities, to the Home Arranger. After a trial period evidence from the test branches indicated that the concept worked and appealed to customers. The big question was the likely impact of the additional workload at branch level.

UNEXPECTED CONSEQUENCES

I have always believed that life is a balance. If you add to one side of the scales there will be a compensating shift on the other side. The introduction of the Home Arranger followed this theory but in an unexpected and dramatic way.

Bob called all the HOFO's to a meeting where we were told that the shift to home ownership would mean that the branch network would be focused on the ability to attract and retain mortgage business. Savings would still be an essential part of funding but would rank behind mortgages. He reasoned that other forms of funding such as the wholesale market made the business less reliant on savings.

This meant that our task was to close a number of branches that didn't meet the new focus on lending. I was given a bunch of statistics providing historical information on the business trends relating to each of our branches. We also had indirect access to a new tool called GMAP that was used by retailers to locate stores. I returned to the office and briefed David. We waded through the pile of information. Looking at current business was straightforward but trying to forecast future business was far more difficult. Forecasting the loss of business following a closure was a real gamble. We now know that customers of closed branches are very likely to close their savings account and take their business elsewhere even when there is another branch in close proximity. Hindsight is a wonderful thing.

Over the next couple of months we closed eight branches, three of which were in Northern Ireland. The impact on staff was huge. David, Alison (Personnel) and I visited all eight branches in person to break the news to staff and tell them what they could expect for the future. It was a very difficult and moving experience feeling the staff's anger and frustration particularly in Northern Ireland where there were very few opportunities to relocate staff. There was also a clearly negative reaction from customers. As each branch closed, huge amounts of money left the Leeds. So much money fled that a new savings account was launched at a very competitive rate. This did help stem the flow, but at a great cost. So much for alternative funding!

ALL THE FUN OF THE FAIR

More changes were planned at HO and positive communication was required. The Leeds had never held a conference outside of Leeds but Blackpool was now the destination for all branch and Head Office senior staff. We considered ourselves fortunate that the conference was to be held in our Area. I decided to make use of the event by holding a half-day Area meeting for all our branch managers and area staff on the last day.

There must have been approaching a thousand staff at the conference spread across a range of hotels. It was held in the aging Norbreck Castle Hotel on the sea front. It had seen better days and someone swore they had seen adverts for rooms to rent BY THE HOUR.

I drove up the M6 in my pride and joy, a Vauxhall Carlton

CDX, accompanied by my PA Lorna. I was running a little late when I heard a siren followed by flashing blue lights as a police car raced up behind me. It overtook - was I going to get away with it? No chance, he cut in front and signalled for me to slow down to a halt on the hard shoulder. I was booked for speeding at 80 mph. Fair cop. I entered the conference reception to gales of laughter and applause from my many colleagues who had driven past on the motorway and witnessed my booking.

The conference itself focused on restructuring at HO and further cost cutting. CEO Mike Blackburn also took the opportunity to deny all rumours of his departure. He famously declared, "I'm not going anywhere" as he disappeared in white smoke to the sound of Tina Turner singing 'Simply The Best'. Reaction was mixed with more concern being expressed by HO staff. Our managers seemed to be as upbeat as usual.

The next morning I chaired our Area meeting where I witnessed a few participants fighting their hangovers. There was also some fun at the expense of one or two who had been seen enjoying themselves perhaps a little too openly swerving across the seafront, but it was all good-natured banter.

For those of us who played golf we moved on to the local municipal course, which was in surprisingly good condition. I played with Peter Maskrey and John Mitchell. Every time I saw John I was reminded of when Barry Walsh (Ellesmere Port and Chester manager) invited him to a Building Society Institute dinner as a late replacement. As a then young trainee John turned up to the black tie event dressed in what looked like his grandad's dinner jacket with lapels that reached passed his arms. References to the godfather came thick and fast but he took it all with good humour.

After leaving school Peter had been a student at a college in Blackpool and knew the area well. On the first hole he stood back admiring the beautiful detached houses surrounding the green and pronounced "I would have to sell my A**SE to be able to afford one of those".

About three hours later when the houses came back into view from the other side of the course John halted play, walked up to Peter, looked at the impressive houses and said, "What sort of HORSE have you got to sell?". Peter and I collapsed to the floor clutching our clubs. John did not understand why we were falling about. It took us a while to regain our composure enough to explain his misunderstanding of Peter's AR**E.

Since that day it is now compulsory for that incident to be retold every May at our continuing Rhosneigr annual reunions.

BACK TO SCHOOL

I have always enjoyed attending courses and was delighted to accept an invitation from HO Training department to join a new financial services course at Manchester Business School. They wanted to test it out and I was to be accompanied by Roger Harrison, a respected HO trainer.

I caught a train from Holmes Chapel into Manchester and met up with Roger at the business school. We were expecting a mixed group of participants but were surprised to discover that we were the only Brits on the course. There were ten people from a Turkish bank of which only half spoke good English. One of the four had an American accent although he had never set foot outside Turkey. He explained that he watched a lot of American TV.

There were two chaps from different African banks. One made it clear early on that he was only attending the course to enable him to buy a second-hand car and ship it home where he would sell it at a profit. He proudly claimed he did this every year as did many of his colleagues at his bank. The other African had tribal scars on his face possibly signifying that in other circles he was a Chief. The two never spoke to each other. There was a chap working for Lloyds Bank in Brazil who took great delight in telling us how dangerous it was working in a branch in that part of world, and that the branches he managed had permanent armed guards.

The course lasted just short of three weeks with four days in the middle spent in the Yorkshire Dales. At the end of each other day we were given a business case to review and comment on as homework. The two Africans never touched them and failed to participate in any meaningful way. Roger and I gave it our best and I enjoyed it, although as an effective financial services course it was hard to recommend. I am sure Roger took that message back to HO.

The four days in the Dales was good fun apart from the caving. Some exercises were open to all of us including a night task where we all got lost. The final exercise was based on our own fears. We had to declare what we were afraid of and try to confront our terrors. I readily admitted that I was a little claustrophobic. That turned out to be a mistake. I was assigned to the cave group. Not one to shirk at participation I decided to give it my best. I was doing ok until the point at which the top of the cave scraped my head. The guide declared that we were approaching "the chimney". To my disappointment this was not one that went up to the cloudless sky above, it was a very narrow horizontal flat tunnel just high and wide enough for head and shoulders. He also mentioned we would need to pass through some puddles of water and that once we started there would be no possibility of turning back. That was enough for me and another chap to opt out. I knew my limits. One of the Africans volunteered to lead the group with the boy from Brazil at the rear. I felt a bit of a failure especially when three of the Turkish ladies eagerly lined up to take part.

The other 'failure' and I watched them set off, crawling on their stomachs into the tiny tunnel that would stretch for about forty feet. It wasn't long before a few startled cries turned to screams from the ladies. It was now too late for them to turn back. I'm not sure how, but they all emerged at the other end. We later learnt that the ladies hadn't fully understood what the guide had said, and had no idea how tough it would be. Another lesson learned: always make sure you fully understand at the outset any task you are set.

CELEBRATING SUCCESS

The Area team was still growing, as were our business results across the board. It was very rewarding to witness everyone's hard work paying off. I was particularly pleased to see some of our talented managers such as Ken Brown and Colin Kemp receiving deserved promotion. There were many others including young trainees such as Gordon Edwards, Stuart Fearns and Russell Dodd being appointed to their first branch as Managers.

The old North West region had established a great reputation for celebrating. We continued this and hosted many social events at Fiddlers Ferry, as well as organising car treasure hunts and games evenings. Morale was high and it was a pleasure to be a part of it. Sadly it was all about to change.

SUMMONED

The call from David Jarratt (Assistant General Manager) came out of the blue. He told me that they were creating a new role in Group Marketing under newly appointed Judy Atchison who had joined from Rank Hovis McDougall where she was marketing director. He was a bit short on detail but stressed that it was a great opportunity. I discussed it with Sue, who after five years in one place, was now very settled. All three children were now at school but still very young with Stephen the eldest, only eight. A move to Leeds would be a challenge.

The next day I went back to David for more details. I had checked the house prices and was surprised to see they were higher in the popular north Leeds area. When I asked about the salary I was even more surprised to hear David say there would be no increase. I didn't want to appear uninterested but the thought of uprooting the family and being financially worse off did not seem right. I calmly explained to David that I could not move to Leeds without a reasonable increase in salary. My resistance paid off as he soon came back with a good offer that helped make the move possible. Sue could see the opportunity for me and also realised that a move was likely at some point and would be even more difficult when the children were older.

A BIT OF A DO

I was delighted that my ASM and good friend David was appointed to take over my role. His promotion was fully deserved and after two years of hard work I was pleased to know that the Area would remain in excellent hands and our staff would be well looked after. It also meant we could have a double celebration at Fiddlers Ferry.

It was a memorable night particularly when the Area ladies, dressed in matching black outfits and dark glasses, performed "the Duffin rap". I was sorry to leave such wonderful people behind but was excited to move on to a new challenge.

OFF TO PROVIDE A SERVICE

Those five years based in Warrington with the jump from managing twenty branches to over sixty with all the added responsibilities had taught me so much. I had gone from managing teams remotely, to leading a large team of Senior Managers. Looking back it went better than I could have hoped. Involvement in experimenting with new ideas and helping to formulate strategy had been exciting. Building an excellent team was vital to our success and I had learnt how to compensate for my own relative weaknesses by developing expertise amongst the staff.

My new role was to be Head of Marketing Services. On the face of it, it looked like I was being given all the areas that didn't really fit in anywhere else. I would soon find out.

CHAPTER 9
HEAD OF MARKETING SERVICES LEEDS
JUNE 1991 TO JUNE 1992

LEEDS

Leeds owes much of its growth from a small manorial borough in the 14th century to a prosperous trading centre in the 18th to the production of woollen cloth. With the Industrial Revolution Leeds developed further with transport, commerce and engineering, earning its City status in 1893. Today it is the fourth largest city in the country with a population of over 750,000. It has a diverse economy with 77% of its working population employed in the private sector. It has also become the largest legal and financial centre outside of London.

PERMANENT HOUSE (HO)

The Leeds' Head Office was situated on The Headrow in the centre of the city. I had visited many times before but this time was different. I was now part of the establishment. I drove into the under cover car park and was greeted by the garage supervisor Steve Smith who fortunately recognised me. It was always a tight squeeze getting into the car park as it was clearly not originally built for this purpose but Steve found me a space and I eased my Carlton CDX into a corner.

As I made my way to the first floor where the Senior Management were housed, I had a moment of misgivings. Was I going to miss the day to day involvement I had enjoyed for the last seventeen years? Would I cope with the politics people talked about when working here? Or would I enjoy my new role as much as I had hoped?

BOB TO THE RESCUE

The first person I met was my previous boss Bob Humphreys. He welcomed me into his office with a cheery smile. I had been expecting to be greeted by Commercial Director, Chris

Chadwick or Head of Marketing, Judy Atchison. Neither of them were there but Bob proved to be an excellent stand in. Within half an hour he had found me an office and introduced me to my new PA Sarah Milner. Sarah was young and bubbly, if a little nervous, but that soon passed. It was a bit of a shambolic start but Bob had been extremely helpful.

NEW TEAM

It soon became very clear that my new function was indeed a collection of small business areas that needed a home and perhaps a new focus. Two areas that had synergy were Sales Planning (SP) and the Business Analysis Unit (BAU).

The SP unit had previously reported to Bob and was where Sarah had come from. David Nicholson was working mainly on sales with a focus on branch targets, while Iain Mckilveen worked on branch and ATM placement. They were both reliable and hardworking with Dave destined for greater things. Iain was so committed that at one stage I had to insist he took two weeks' holiday as he had built up several weeks' entitlement.

There was also a young lad called Gary in SP who all too frequently turned up with a black eye and I chose to turn a blind one.

The BAU had some very capable analysts including the Manager, Paul Bevan, and his deputy Alan Reeve. There were half a dozen in the team who seemed to be able to pull together any stats you wanted in a format of your choosing. They were a very valuable asset used to good effect by many at HO.

There was also Merchandising, managed by Joyce Anson, which was responsible for marketing support such as giveaways, window displays, leaflets, saving sticks (plastic money box tubes) and much more. Finally there was a one-man operation supporting house builders, the one man being Jim Drake.

Bob informed me that I was to chair the three monthly meetings of the Area Sales Managers. This delighted me, as I knew them all and was keen to stay close to the branch network.

Moving from managing over 400 people via a team of Senior Managers to around a dozen or so more junior grades was very different but I was assured this was all part of my development.

THE NAME'S DRAKE

The part of my new domain that stood out as slightly odd was Jim Drake's builders' support. I can't remember the exact title but essentially The Leeds put aside a substantial amount of mortgage funds to help new house building. The nearest Leeds branch to a new development would be allocated funds in addition to the normal branch allocation. This was known as builders' block allocation. Managing this area and maintaining good relations with the builders was a key part of Jim's role.

Jim had risen through the branch network and in the early 1980s had been seconded to a task force set up by the government minister Michael Heseltine following the Toxteth riots. The effectiveness of the task force was difficult to assess but Jim's participation reflected well on both him and The Leeds.

The highlight of Jim's year was the Builders' Dinner, a lavish affair, which he organised, inviting the leaders of all the main house builders. I only attended once and remembering it being a good do mainly due to Jim's excellent organisational skills.

His office was adjacent to mine and he was always up for a quick chat about football, particularly Leeds United. The rest of the time I left him to manage an area which needed little of my attention.

JUST ONE CORNETTO

It wasn't long before Bob was stretching my role. I didn't mind at all, in fact I was pleased to be involved in new areas. Having the BAU led me to become involved in many interesting projects. Including looking at ways to improve the handling of arrears.

However, responsibility for diverse areas meant that I was dragged into some unlikely situations. One day I was summoned to Bob's office. He informed me that a group of Senior Managers would be arriving from an Italian bank. They were interested in our approach to sales through the branches. Bob told me that my field experience and responsibility for sales planning made me an ideal candidate to present to them. I was excited by the prospect and pleased when Bob handed me a hard copy of a set of slides for me to use. This was going to be a doddle I thought!

The delegation from the Bank of Venice sat attentively as Frank Burroughs from Planning went through his slides on Corporate Planning. They were pretty non-committal, which I found unsettling. Bob wasn't there so Roger Gray from Business Operations was facilitating the meeting and introduced me. The slides Bob had given me were ones he had used internally to sell the sales concept. It was entitled "Hunters and Skinners". The basic concept was that branch counter staff found the sales leads (Hunters) and referred the customers to sales staff to complete the sale (Skinners). As soon as the first slide went up displaying the cartoon cavemen to depict the Hunters and Skinners, I felt the temperature drop ten degrees and our guests begin to shuffle. Despite my unease I had no choice but to continue with the presentation. When I got to the end and invited questions. Roger's face was a picture.

The most senior Italian banker felt the need to ask at least one question. "How successful has this been?" he asked with a look of disdain on his face. I tried to look confident and replied, "It's early days, but the proof of the pudding is in the eating". I knew before the words had passed my lips that this was a mistake. Shoulders were shrugged, eyebrows were raised and the bankers huddled together whispering in their native tongue. Roger took over and brought the meeting to a hasty close. Our guests thanked us for our hospitality and promised to invite us to their bank. I am still waiting for the invitation. Another lesson learned: know your audience and adapt accordingly.

THE GOLDEN TRIANGLE

Yet another house move beckoned and I was straight on the case. Virtually everyone I asked recommended the golden triangle. This was the popular area between Harrogate, Wetherby and Boston Spa. Now that Sue's Mum was part of the equation we needed an extra room narrowing the selection somewhat.

One of the ASMs, Chris Kelly, had recently moved to Edinburgh from Wetherby. His house was still on the market and had the benefit of a ground floor extension that was ideal for Sue's Mum. This seemed to be an opportunity not to be missed so the deal was done quickly. We had accepted an offer on our house back in Cheshire, albeit at a price below the one we had paid two years before.

IN THE CHAIR

My first ASMs meeting had gone smoothly and I was looking forward to the next one that would be held at the Yorkshire Area office in my new home town of Wetherby.

The ASMs were a lively but usually disciplined group. The meeting had gone well when one of the Area office staff popped in and handed a written message to the nearest ASM. That was Colin Kemp who I had known well from his time in the North West at Ellesmere Port and before that at Walsall in the Midlands. On Colin's right hand side was Chris Kelly who had sold us his house in Wetherby. Colin read the note and passed it to the ASM on his left. He read it and passed it on to his left. They missed me out but the note went all the way round the other ASM's until it was eventually handed to Chris Kelly. It turned out the note was confirming Chris's holiday booking. There was much laughter and Chris took it all in his good-humoured stride.

I enjoyed these meetings mainly because they enabled me to bring members of my team to brief the ASM's on marketing support and still feel close to the branch network.

HEAD IN HANDS

I am not sure how it happened but in the Spring I was invited to a dinner organised by the Leeds Chamber of Commerce with the then Prime Minister John Major as guest speaker. The PM was a keen sports fan and supported Chelsea FC. One of the speakers made a derogatory comment about his club and he theatrically put his head in his hands. The audience laughed but the large room was lit up as numerous flash bulbs burst in to life. He was play-acting of course but the next morning the papers blazed the picture across their pages full of the political crisis it was said to portray. You can still find that picture on the Internet.

A PRACTICE RUN

The small Southdown Building Society (SD) located on the south coast was now in financial difficulty. The Leeds decided to come to its rescue. There were two main reasons to help. Firstly someone had to help ensure continued confidence in building societies and it was probably our turn. The second was we were interested in expanding and this would be a useful taste of the process required to merge with or swallow a competitor.

I was dispatched to visit several Southdown branches to help keep up local staff morale. In fact over a period of six months there were many visits from Leeds' Senior Management nearly always staying at the same hotel. Most quickly learnt to request a room at the back of the building but those less savvy were often caught out by being tempted into the larger room at the front. There was a bus stop conveniently situated directly outside the hotel. Unfortunately the front bedroom windows were on the same level as the bus's upstairs windows. More than one Leeds' executive left the safety of their shower only to be greeted by a staring bus passenger. The surprise was mutual.

Three senior Southdown managers; Martin Batt, Paul French and Paul Gilmour joined us in Leeds. The merger went ahead smoothly and confidence for any further mergers was high.

SAVING UP A NEW ROLE

I didn't see this coming. I had struck up a good working relationship with my boss Judy Atchison. She was a professional marketeer who had progressed to the main board at Rank Hovis McDougall before moving to the Leeds. Judy had a serious work ethic accompanied by a tremendous sense of humour.

After being summoned unexpectedly to her office I sat and wondered what this was about. Judy informed me that the Head of Savings, David Andrew would be leaving and she wanted me to take over. David had not been with the Leeds long. During his time, savings had been under pressure following the round of branch closures and the impact of several privatisations, which had sucked money from savings accounts.

This was a much bigger challenge for me that would raise my profile and add greatly to my business experience. I was lifted by the confidence Judy had in me and excited by the prospect.

ONE LAST LESSON

I had been in my current role for less than a year, but I had learnt a lot. I now knew how HO worked. I had attended the fortnightly Executive Directors' briefings and played a full role in Chris Chadwick's quarterly commercial reviews.

As Marketing Services was a new function, I was asked to help with the drafting of a new job specification and person profile to aid recruitment. This was done by interview. A chap, who shall remain nameless, spent a couple of hours making notes from my honest answers to his questions. Near the end he asked me if there were any real difficulties and to name names where problems had arisen. He assured me this was for "context" only. It was to help him understand my answers and would not be disclosed. I went ahead on the strict understanding that he would keep to his word.

Within twenty-four hours I was summoned to a General Manager's office for a humiliating dressing down. I was livid. I returned to my office and picked up the phone demanding the return of the super grass. He appeared and sheepishly sat down. I told him that I didn't hold grudges but was prepared to make an exception in his case and told him to leave and never darken my door again. I had never felt like this before and fortunately I never did again.

CHAPTER 10
HEAD OF SAVINGS
JUNE 1992 TO JUNE 1995

EVEN SMALLER

My new team was the smallest I had managed since my days
in Cannock more than ten years earlier. There were just eight
of us, nine if you counted the Youth Training Scheme (YTS)
girl. The marketing manager was Carolyn Holroyd. She was a
very experienced, tall dark haired thirty something and the real
hub of the team. There were four product managers with Doug
Mackenzie, and Duncan McKay looking after the main
products including Liquid Gold, Solid Gold and Bonus Gold;
Andrea Stoker supported travel money, Young Leeder and
share dealing; leaving Andrew Moss to care for the London
professional's account, Tessa Gold and Leeds Overseas
(based in the Isle of Man).

My new PA was Cath Shearn. Slimly built with fair hair, she
was very quiet compared with my previous PA the bubbly
Sarah Milner, but an effective administrative assistant to both
Carolyn and myself. Nicola Watson also provided clerical
support to the rest of the team.

ANOTHER LANGUAGE

On my first morning I was pleasantly surprised to learn that
biscuits were regularly supplied at coffee time. The ninth
member of our team, (I will call her Jenny), our YTS recruit
stood with a look of dismay on her young face. The Savings
team shared the cost of very nice biscuits with the coins kept
in an ornate Oxo tin. "Where is the money '*fut*' biscuits?" she
enquired. Cath looked across and pointed at the coin holder.
The youngster picked it up and shook it but there was no
sound. "*t'int tin tin*" she exclaimed in her strong Leeds accent.
The inevitable laughter was not what she expected, poor
thing. Cath quickly passed the tin around for reloading and
soon our little helper was off to the shops.

As time went on Cath began to teach Jenny some secretarial skills and her confidence grew. Soon after she had begun to take phone messages she went to Cath and tried to explain a message she had taken. "What did they say?" asked Cath. Communication wasn't Jenny's strong point and she quickly became exasperated, as she was not finding it easy to get the facts across. Eventually she drew breath and said *"whar' it were, were…."* then defeated, stopped and went off in a huff. The English language murdered again. Not that I can say much with my Brummie accent.

IS IT A PLANT?

My new office was on the same floor as previously but I was now close to the office of the CEO Mike Blackburn and his PA Barbara Plant. Mike had many visitors particularly the other executive directors including the IT director John Miller. John had suspiciously dark brown hair, as did Barbara. There were those who began to see a connection and very soon a spotting game began. Were John and Barbara one and the same person, as spookily they never seemed to be seen at the same time? Silly I know but the speculation went on for quite a while until one day the spell was broken when they left Mikes room together. It was concluded that they simply used the same hair dye.

IT'S A RAID

Work on our new Head Office at Lovell Park was progressing well. The first area to be completed was the Security Control Centre (SCC). All of Judy's team were invited over for a demonstration of the state of the art technology, rumoured to be costing over three million pounds.

We all looked a bit silly as we stood in the control room wearing our hard hats that were deemed necessary due to the unfinished building work. The SSC manager explained that the Leeds had gone from virtually no security to a leading edge position. Every single branch was wired in to the same technology as Fort Knox where the USA stores its gold. There were strategically placed sensors and alarm buttons strategically all of over. Mr SCC was keen to demonstrate the new technology and asked for a volunteer. Judy quickly raised her hand. He went on to simulate a raid on a branch.

He asked Judy to give the nod for the exact time for the raid to begin. We waited, expecting to be spellbound by the results. Just as Judy was about to give the signal, loud alarms began to shrill. "It's a raid, it's a raid!" the manager shouted excitedly. "It is not a simulated raid for the members of the executive, it is real raid!" His excitement was contagious. Using the state of the art communication system he declared the name of the branch, and his team immediately got on to checking the authenticity of the raid. It was actually genuine, but amazingly once the raid location was identified Security Control just alerted the police and stood back.

Calm returned, we removed out hard hats and shuffled back to our offices on The Headrow. We couldn't help feeling a little disappointed that our £3 million had been spent on a super efficient detection system which resulted in rather low key action, similar in fact to a member of branch staff noticing a raid and dialing 999.

PLANS AFOOT

I was determined to make full use of my branch experience and connections in my new role. Ideas were forming particularly the treatment of past issues. These were accounts that were no longer on offer to new customers but were still live but paying interest rates well below current products. This unfairly penalised those who did not keep up to date and I was determined to rectify such a poor practice.

After just a few days in the job the in-house newspaper "The Leeder" sent John Hanlon to interview me. He wrote a piece under the title "New Savings Chief's Pledge". I really didn't have much to contribute so I played safe and focused on my team developing closer links with branches to understand the issues that concerned both staff and customers. I also drew on the well used phrase "evolution not revolution". It was fair to say I was playing for time.

THAT'S LIFE

Many of the Leeds' competitors were busy creating their own Life companies. The Leeds also decided this was a good move and began assembling a team to launch Leeds Life. This was going to have an impact on Savings as it would create competition for funds. I was on the outside of the project team but keeping a close eye on progress.

Rumours were rife about who was going to be appointed to lead the project. It turned out to be Ladislav Suchopar who joined from Allied Dunbar. A story circulated that he was interviewed by several senior managers and directors and at the end of the session he stood up and announced that he would return in thirty minutes when he would expect to receive their decision. Ballsy but it clearly worked!

Just after joining he was introduced to some of the Assistant General Managers (AGMs). It was reported that one of them commented that Ladislav was an unusual name and asked if they could call him "Laddie". He instantly replied "If you are not comfortable with Ladislav you can call me Sir!".

In fairness the project was a success and Leeds Life launched on time. Throughout the development of the project I had often noticed everyone standing at their team meetings. Apparently they had been instructed to do this to avoid the meetings becoming over long. Thankfully the impact on savings balances was minimal.

ANDY RETURNS TO THE FOLD

In another part of the insurance area they were gearing up for the new regulations affecting sales. As a result new trainers were recruited and amongst them my very good friend Andy Bates returned to the business after a couple of years in

Norfolk. Andy and his wife Terri moved into a new house, not far from us in nearby Knaresborough. It was great to have our close friends back. Andy told me the location was temporary while they looked for something more suitable, but nearly thirty years later they are still there.

SHOCK DEPARTURE

Despite his earlier denial, Mike Blackburn resigned in February 1993 to join the Halifax as CEO. Nobody could blame him, as he had been made an offer too good to refuse. In his time at The Leeds he had achieved a real change and left the business in good shape. The news of his departure left us all wondering what would happen next.

The big question was who would take over at the helm. The immediate solution was the temporary appointment of finance director Roger Boyes as acting CEO. The prospect of another more significant merger seemed not only possible, but a probable long term solution.

ON THE MOVE

Our new Head Office at Lovell Park or "Lovely Park" as it became affectionately known, was completed in 1993 and Judy's team were one of the first to move in. I had a smart spacious office on the first floor with an area at one end of my long desk suitable for hosting meetings. It was a far cry from my windowless cupboard back in Cannock. The building was very contemporary in design, with air conditioning that worked, and strange tubes that linked the office to the car park. It was a bit "Star Trek" except you stayed visible!

Next door to my office was my colleague Charles Wycks who, as Head of Lending, also reported to my boss Judy Atchison. Charles was always immaculately dressed. I put this down to his early training as a tailor's apprentice (or maybe a sorcerer's apprentice) after leaving school. His reddish brown hair was cut short and never appeared to grow at all. Some were convinced it was a wig, but the truth was he went to the hairdressers so regularly that it never had time to grow.

He was a good friend and colleague and we often shared a good laugh and enjoyed talking football. One important thing Charles taught me was how to convince people you were still at work when actually you had left for home. Every night he would leave his jacket draped over the back of his office chair. No matter how late I stayed Charles appeared to be working later! It fooled me for weeks until I realised what he was up to.

MERGER ANNOUNCED

On the 4th August 1993 the news many of us expected, a merger, was announced. The Leeds was to merge with the National and Provincial Building Society who were based in nearby Bradford. They were about two thirds the size of the Leeds but their CEO David O'Brien (DOB) was to take charge of the new entity, filling the gap left by Mike Blackburn.

Meetings were soon arranged and I found their approach to Savings very similar to ours. They wanted to remove all their past issues (defunct accounts paying very low rates of interest) and try where possible to put the customer first. I got on with their equivalent of our product managers but was less keen on my counterpart Dr Stephen Clode. He seemed detached from his team and always slightly on edge.

Whilst the Savings merger team was pressing forward, problems were surfacing in other areas. The N&P used some very bizarre phrases to explain how they approached business. So bizarre that no one at the Leeds had a clue what they meant half of the time. Apart from the management spiel I witnessed the powerful effect their CEO could have on his staff when Dr Steve and I were called to present our plans to both CEOs. We had a well thought out plan that included the radical removal of all our combined past issues. I was excited to share this with our leaders, but Dr Steve was so nervous that I have to admit I looked at the floor beneath him expecting a puddle to form. He was shaking. I asked him what the matter was. He nervously replied that if DOB didn't like what we proposed he would eat us for breakfast. I was so confident (some may say cocky!) that I breezed into the room to share our brilliant plans. Dr Steve sidled in behind me and remained virtually silent throughout the presentation. Both CEOs were impressed and gave a favourable reaction. Although I was not keen on the way DOB ran the business I was delighted that at least the Savings area looked to be heading in the right direction.

But rumours regarding both the N&P and DOB continued to circulate. Even the press joined in with negative reports. I was invited to a meeting of senior managers to confront our CEO and a couple of the Leeds' Non- Executive Directors. The feedback from the floor on the merger proposal was extremely negative. Our two cultures were far apart and none of us could see it working. DOB received particular criticism from almost everyone in the room.

THE MERGER IS OFF BUT BOB ISN'T

Soon afterwards it was announced that the merger was off. There was a collective sigh of relief across the business. My old boss Bob Humphreys had experienced a particularly difficult time and was looking forward to some well earned 'R and R' with his wife Sheila at the Executive Christmas dinner, as was I.

Held on the fifth floor at Lovell Park it was a splendid affair with everyone celebrating what many thought was a lucky escape. As drink was aplenty nearly everyone was travelling to and from the event by taxi. Sue and I had arranged to share a taxi with Charles and his wife Helen as they lived in Boston Spa about a mile past Wetherby. I have to admit we had all had at least one too many and spirits were high.

As we stood in a throng of inebriated revelers a steady flow of taxis pulled up outside and came in to hunt for their customers. We stood close to the door and heard, "Boston Spa, Humphreys". Charles and I looked at each other, exchanged smirks and gently pulled our better halves out into the taxi. We giggled like naughty children all the way home.

Back at Lovell Park Bob was soon informed of the hijacking and the names of the culprits. He was not happy at being made to wait even though he quickly picked up the taxi we had ordered for the same journey. No harm done but it doesn't do to out "rank" a former boss.

FUTURE FOR PAST ISSUES LOOKS GOOD

As we entered 1994 N&P wasted no time and removed all of their past issues. They received some good press but I felt they could have made much more of their move. I was determined to do a better job. We had already started extensive research with particular focus on how to communicate with affected customers, and how to brief staff. There would be almost one million customers affected, with combined balances of £850 million. We consulted 4000 of our high balance customers as well as seeking the views of many staff.

We positioned it as a win-win-win, i.e. a great deal for customers, improved business retention and a lift to staff morale. The process went remarkably well and had excellent press coverage: "Three cheers for the good guys" and "A step in the right direction". With this one of my "hobby horses" was put to bed.

ON THE ROAD TO CUSTOMER SEGMENTATION

Roger Ivy's customer database team had been working for months on a cutting edge, and very expensive method of labeling the current and potential value of our customers. It was a complex issue and appeared to be taking forever.

My old boss Bob led a workshop for his HOFOs to explain the project's progress. I was invited along with the rest of Judy's team. I sat in the front row hoping to be able to ask questions, but it quickly became evident that this was a mistake. When Roger Ivy's assistant Gordon Longfellow stood up he uncovered a child's car garage and two toy lorries. I instantly knew I was going to have trouble keeping a straight face right in front of him.

Gordon sounded like Tommy Cooper when he reached down and said "red lorry, yellow lorry". He tried his best to use the lorries to describe the complexity of his task but the titters were relentless and it wasn't long before I completely lost the plot, as did many if not all in the room. Bob pulled us all back to order but from that moment on the project and countless thousands of pounds were lost.

THE BIG ONE

Mike Blackburn had been gone for over eighteen months. The N&P merger had failed. There was still uncertainty in my bones when I was summoned to CEO Roger Boyes's office. I sat down and he got straight to the point. "I am going to ask you to sign a declaration of secrecy" he said seriously. My interest was immediately piqued. What was this? He then started to smile as he told me we were going to merge with the Halifax. He became more and more animated as he added that we would then move on to be launched on the stock exchange as a PLC. I was delighted to be included as one of the 'secret circle' but there was much work to be done in my area before the official announcement. Thankfully I could invite one more of my team to help. I decided to involve Mike Jarvis who had joined a few months earlier and I knew from his days as Wrexham branch manager.

The main reason for secrecy was to avoid people placing large deposits before the official announcement as this would mean they would get more free Halifax shares based on their savings balance on the day of the announcement.

WHO IS IN CHARGE?

Mike and I worked with a senior partner from our lawyers Allen and Overy. As you would expect he was first class and easily adapted to our main task which was to draft the wording relating to Savings in the announcement and work on the guidance instructions for staff at HO and at our branches.

The proposed merger was announced first thing on Friday 25th November 1994 and a wave of uncertainty spread across the staff of The Leeds. Head of IT George Scarlett had previously confirmed that all balances would be recorded and flagged at the time of the announcement. I had spoken to the Halifax to make sure they would be doing the same. They came back to me with the bad news that they would not be able to record and flag balances until a day later. I reminded them that the cut off date and time had now been made public. I reported the problem at my end to let the "grown ups" sort it out.

I worked over the weekend on the staff communications. By Sunday there was only Mike Jarvis and I from Savings, plus George from IT. Thankfully Charles Wycks turned up to offer a helping hand. I had dragged my old PA Sarah in to type all the staff information. We needed 150 copies for HO helplines. I was waiting for a decision on the date. Would it be the originally agreed 25th November 1994, or would we have to settle for the 26th to meet the Halifax IT constraints? Sarah typed two versions to cover both dates. Eventually I received a call from above instructing me to go with the Halifax date. At this point it became clear as to who was to be in charge. It was the West team, not the East team (East and West were the code names used during negotiations).

"LIKE JOINING THE CIVIL SERVICE"

In the middle of 1993 product managers Doug and Duncan decided to seek pastures new. My boss Judy wanted us to recruit a talented marketer and Jane Bellhouse joined us from Boots. It was obvious that she had benefitted from a classic marketing background, unlike mine.

When we started to work with the Halifax it quickly became clear that there was a clash in approach. The Halifax sent over Paul Williams, their savings guru. Paul was a couple of years younger than me and also from Birmingham, although his accent was even more pronounced than mine. Paul and Jane didn't get on. The marketer verses the pragmatist, both bright and determined but from very different worlds.

Part of the problem was that the Halifax was well organised but more like the civil service than a modern business. They ran their branches along tick box processes called "key controls". Sales and customer focus were way down the pecking order. I could see why my old CEO Mike was keen to rock the Halifax boat and this was certainly happening.

BLINDED BY THE LIGHT

It was time for a diversion from the merger. We had a very good relationship with many of our suppliers, which sometimes led to an invitation to a sporting event. In the summer of 1995 I was given two tickets to the Open golf at St Andrews, the Scottish home of golf. I decided to invite my good friend and keen golfer Dennis Skinner to join me.

We were only going for the day. That meant a very early start to be there long enough to enjoy the golf. We set off at about 4.30am. It was a clear day and I put my foot down as there was very little traffic on the roads. I should have paid closer attention to the speed limits in some of the small villages, but we were virtually on our own.

Dennis had sat quietly for the first couple of hours but the latest camera flash stirred him to comment, "that's the third time you have been flashed for speeding" he said without a smile. "Two more and you will lose your licence". He was right of course, and I tried hard to slow down but it was difficult at 6am with no sign of traffic to match.

By the time we pulled up in the car park at St Andrews I was trying to come to terms with losing my licence as we had received two more flashes. Five lots of three points would be more than enough to put me off the road for a few months.

The golf was good and we returned home in normal traffic

conditions with no camera flashes. Back in 1994 the speed cameras used traditional film, not like today's digital cameras. Unbelievably I did not receive one ticket. Lucky me!

NEARING THE END

The two Savings teams were making good progress, with Halifax agreeing to follow our lead on past issues. However there were some trip ups in the negotiations.

One of the meetings of senior executives was held on the oak panelled fourth floor in Halifax. Once everyone was settled a member of the Leeds team rose to serve coffee. The Halifax team told him politely to stay seated as the coffee would be served by the white-gloved catering staff. The Leeds chap continued towards the coffee trolley cheerfully pointing out that they poured coffee for each other at The Leeds. "No! No!" came the shouts, but it was too late. As the trolley was dragged away from the wall it became apparent that the jugs were plugged into the wall. The coffee and hot milk went everywhere, up the wall and all over the bright yellow carpet. Our man was highly embarrassed but somehow managed to stay clear of the erupting liquid.

PARTY TIME

I was lucky enough to be invited to two "End of the Leeds" parties. There was spectacular one held at Harewood House for HO staff. There were all sorts of entertainment including a tethered hot air balloon and a spectacular firework display to end a marvellous evening.

The other party was held at a hotel in Warrington for my old North West Area colleagues. My old friend Andy Bates had also been invited so we booked a room and drove over.

It was great to meet up with so many people but I was soon in trouble. Standing at the bar I recognised a couple of young ladies. I said hello and spotted that one of them appeared to be pregnant. I casually asked when the happy event was expected only to be told, "I had the baby four weeks ago". Luckily she smiled and tried to reassure me that she was not offended.

I was enjoying the excellent live band when I was dragged to the stage and told I was going to perform. Fortunately, all I had to do was stand in front of the lead guitarist and put my hands behind my back. He then threaded his hands around me and placed his guitar in front of me. The effect was remarkable as it now looked as though I was playing like a pro. I tried to move with the music shaking my head in time. The audience went along with it as I bowed to their applause at the end.

As the drinks were free I made an early decision to stick to shandy. Unfortunately the decision was lost on Andy and unbeknown to me I was drinking full strength on his rounds. I paid the price next day. After the official closing time we stayed in the hotel bar area singing along as David Cook tinkled the ivories.

HALIFAX BOUND

Confirmation of my role as Assistant General Manager for Savings came through. In line with everyone else my salary stayed fixed with a promise to review it in six months' time. I was to be based in Dean Clough where the Halifax Savings team was housed. It was an old building (circa 1840) that many years previously had been the home of Crossley Carpets. As I drove into the car park it reminded me of Charles Dickens' book Hard Times. I was certainly hoping they wouldn't be.

EPILOGUE

My twenty-one years with the Leeds had prepared me well for life at the Halifax. I was also very fortunate to still be reporting to Judy, as was Charles as AGM Mortgages. This meant we had a much easier time than the majority of our Leeds colleagues who went through massive changes.

I stayed with the Halifax for the next seven years before retiring due to the loss of much of my sight in 2002. I had kept Savings under my wing but when I left I had added Mortgages to my portfolio.

It was sad to see the impact of the financial crisis on the business. But I try not to look back too often. Would life have been better if the Leeds had ploughed on alone? It is, of course impossible to say and most opinions are probably heavily influenced by how the merger affected them as individuals.

I worked with some very good people at the Halifax particularly Mike Ellis who gave me tremendous support and encouragement and of course Judy Atchison. I also had a great team of bright loyal people with me including Judith Cork, David Roberts, Phil Jenks and Ian Stewart.

For another nine years after retirement I sat on the board of the HBOS Foundation. You were supposed to only do a three-year term but I was delighted to help out for so long. It was very rewarding to see the help we could give to such deserving causes. The staff input was incredible and attending the annual awards night was a humbling yet enjoyable experience.

As my sight and hearing continue to slowly deteriorate, I am grateful to still be able to write with the aid of modern technology and now move onwards toward the fourth book.

APPENDIX 1
OTHER AMUSING LEEDS STORIES I RECEIVED (PUBLISHED AS WRITTEN WITH ONLY VERY LIGHT EDITING)

JOHN MOSELEY

Sheffield was quite a big branch, with a lot of post, but no franking machine. This was deemed an expensive and unnecessary luxury, so each individual letter sent was duly recorded in a post book with a note as to whether it was first or second class (usually second) and the cost of the postage. Thus there was no way to smuggle my three or four letters through this impressively secure system. Anyway the lady that controlled the postbook hated me and would have grassed me up immediately. I doubt even knowing the first and last names of the board of directors would have saved me, so I went cap in hand to my branch manager's office, knelt before him and asked if I might include the copies of minutes that absolutely needed to be posted in the branch post. He sucked his breath in through his teeth and muttered something about it being "highly irregular." I countered that I was only in this position because he had asked me to "get involved with the BSI" but if he would prefer I would present the BSI with a bill for four postage stamps each month? This had the desired effect. I think he could see all those extra BSI Annual Dinner tickets flying to the competitors' arms at the Nationwide or wherever. He told me to leave it with him.

I heard nothing for about a week. Then I received a phone call from one of the four Assistant General Managers of the society a Mr Germaine (Edward Spencer if you are interested – see, it never leaves you!). I gulped. "What have I done wrong?" I thought. This must be pretty serious. Now Edward Spencer Germaine was highly irregular himself. For one he liked to be known as "Ted" by everyone from the cleaners upwards. No "sir" handle for this guy, Self-styled champion the workers he was universally popular, among the proletariat anyway. Even so an AGM phoning me? I took the receiver with some trepidation. I think he probably understood the impact his call might have. He was friendly to a fault, asked me how I was getting on and had obviously taken the trouble to find out a couple of snippets about me. He told of course it was OK to use a bit of postage to support the BSI and if anyone had a problem with it to refer them to him. After a few more pleasantries our call ended.

I rather inadvisably told my branch manager about the call. It did not go down well but I was only 18. With a few more years on my back I might just have omitted the name dropping. Interesting though that a General Manager was required to approve expenditure of around £2 a month in today's money. As I say the Leeds in its heyday didn't believe in spending anything that it didn't have

MARK WATERHOUSE

I came over to Paul's region in Warrington to give the "State of the nation" address to your staff and they all went down with food poisoning. I'd moved on to do the same presentation the following day to the South West and South Wales and Thames Valley regions and you tried tracking me down to check I was alright which luckily I was.

In terms of more amusing stories, apart from many a great night out with Roger Gray and Phil O'Connor, which I'm sure you will know about most of these, relate to my time in Mortgage accounts in the late seventies. There was a great character there called Peter Gabbidon who unfortunately is no longer with us but his antics have gone down in history. Like when at the height of the troubles in Northern Island we had to evacuate Albion House because there was a ticking noise coming from a bag left in the gents toilet on the first floor. Only when the police said it was alarm clock did Peter remember it was his and he'd picked it up from the repairers but had left it in the toilet by accident. Then there was the time he bumped off work and was seen by thousands on TV as he stopped play when he walked behind the bowlers arm distracting the batsman. Or the time he reported his car stolen from the car park to the police only to get home and find he'd left it on his drive that day and got the bus into work.

One other story I remember was me sitting in the Leeds head office canteen with John Hanlon, who you will remember was the editor of the Leeder staff magazine with Peter Crowther for many years. We both commented on the number of "suits" in the canteen and pledged we'd never end up like them and that we were only seeing this job as a temporary position. We were both 16 at the time and these so-called suits were probably only about 18 and both John and I went on to have very long careers with the Leeds/Halifax with John retiring a couple of years ago after 40 years' service.

JULIE WALKER-PYGOTT (GREEN)

For me personally the merger was THE most stressful part of my career when I look back! I had recently been appointed as one of the Savings Customer Service Assistant Managers and had been in role approx 2 months when the merger was announced! Part of my role was managing the Helpdesk and our call volumes went from 1000 calls per day (average) to 14,000 overnight with still the same number of staff-absolute nightmare and my boys were still only 7 and 4 at that time!

No one had any answers and we were quickly given scripts which I believe came from you and Alan and Avery Sols who were acting Solicitors at the time. The scripts changed constantly as did the barrage of questions asked of us and I remember hot footing it up to your office several times a day with the newest questions being asked! Investors were understandably very irate and demanded answers we simply couldn't provide! It became apparent the existing 20 or so staff could not cope with the ever-increasing volumes of calls so a temporary Helpdesk was set up in Bristol of all places- very handy-not! Rumour had it the shabby looking building was in fact a disused cow shed that had been given a lick of paint and equipped with around 100 or so temps who knew nothing about Building Societies let alone savings rates etc! The idea was they would take on the easy calls and work from a script leaving the Savings team in Leeds to handle the more complex calls and vast amount of written enquiries too!

It was quickly apparent that the Bristol set up needed some support so myself and a couple of colleagues Colin Gath and Steve Lee were asked to go to Bristol, this became a regular occurrence in the early days. One lasting memory for me was whilst listening in to some incoming calls I began to feel unwell, I woke up outside laid flat out on a wall, I had apparently fainted! I can still visualise all the tressle tables set out row after row with temps crammed in to the max, think it just finished me off haha!

It was a difficult period for staff as the Leeds/Halifax teams were slowly integrated and job uncertainty was at its prime. The Leeds appeared very forward thinking and when we were shown Halifax policy and procedures it was like going back in time 10 years!

The best part of the entire merger however was the huge farewell party at Harewood House- wow what a night that was, we certainly went out in style that's for sure!

ALAN TODD

One mildly amusing anecdote from my time at the Leeds was when I worked for Arthur Haycock in Southport. He expected his coffee served every day at precisely 10:00 am, and tea at precisely 3:00pm - military style punctuality!

One particular day his secretary Sue Coombs must have been too busy to serve tea exactly on schedule and Arthur pointed this out to her so she duly obliged and made his tea. Rather than wait for the kettle to boil she ran the hot tap until it was as hot as possible, put a tea bag in the cup, and filled it straight from the tap.

As far as I know Arthur never noticed the difference, nor ever found out how it was made.

MARK JESSOP

Back in the mortgage completions days we used to have a good game whereby we'd choose a random band at the start of the day. We'd then try to get their song titles into conversations with branches, solicitors and customers.

PETER MASKREY

Rings a bell

1980 and I am Area Rep in Chester. The Leeds branch was very small but extremely busy and was situated on Eastgate Street right under the famous clock on the bridge that carries the City Wall path over the road.
The manager's office was on the ground floor and was also small but had a bookcase built into the wall. The bookcase, however, had a secret! It was hinged and a hidden lever meant you could pull it out from the wall to reveal a hidden space which contained a trap door that lead to a ladder down to the foundations of a Roman Guardhouse half way under the road almost directly under the Clock. It was just like an Agatha Christie novel and this is absolutely true!! Part of the lease on the premises stated that although we didn't need to advertise the fact, any member of the public could gain access and ask to view the Roman remains.
It never happened!

Then one day I returned to the branch at lunch time after making my calls to the professional community (mainly solicitors and bankers) and there in the banking hall stood one of the Leed's Assistant General Managers, Ian Bell together with an oldish professorial looking man. I recognised Ian Bell and went and greeted him and he introduced me to Dr T Harrington a Director of the Leeds. He asked where the

manager, John Andrews was and I told him he was at lunch (he was in the City Arms on Frodsham Street lunching with the professional community as he did most days and the lunch was primarily liquid but that's how it was in those days).
He told me that I would do (it's nice to feel important!) and could I show Dr Harrington the Roman remains because he was excited to see them.

This I did and we both emerged covered in dust and cobwebs with dead flies and other insects attached to them. Great news for my new suit.

Ian Bell then asked where they could have lunch and I told them there was a brasserie in the basement of the Grosvenor Hotel next door which was pretty good. Lead the way he said to me and I now found myself with these two important people (to a lowly young Rep like me) in the Grosvenor Hotel with a menu in my hand.
Dr Harrington suddenly exclaims that they have frogs' legs on the menu and asks me if I have ever tried frogs legs.
Obviously, a simple answer of "no" was too easy for me and in my nervousness and being eager to please I remembered an old Bernard Manning joke and said, "Well I tried them once but I didn't like them, they kept kicking the peas off the plate."
Silence and for a moment the brasserie turned to black and white, no-one moved and tumbleweed blew through the restaurant.
I was pretty quiet for the rest of the time worrying where my career was heading.

Six months later the branch achieved £1 million gross receipts in a month which was a huge amount of money for those days and the branch was rewarded with one of the two Assistant General Managers taking the whole branch out for a slap up meal. The meal was arranged in the posh restaurant of the Grosvenor and Ian Bell was allocated to host the meal. The wine flowed, tongues loosened, and I held the floor for a few moments and told everyone the story of Ian Bell's last visit and the frogs legs joke. I thought it went down well but when I looked at Ian Bell his face was stony and he just said, "It wasn't funny the first time."

I thought to myself, why can't I ever remember that the secret of digging yourself out of a hole is first to stop digging! I was convinced my fledgling career was over but I was promoted to Branch Manager at Crewe some months later which was just as well as I couldn't see me making it as a stand-up comedian !

Daylight robbery (also from Peter Maskrey)

I was still involved with integrating the two Manchester city centre branches and my PFA (Personal Financial Advisor) for Manchester was Josie Taylor who on the day in question was working at the Moseley Street branch.

Whilst on lunch she went to Lloyds Bank opposite to transact some personal business and was stood behind a man in the middle of robbing the bank and holding a gun on the cashier. He was doing it all very surreptitiously and the cashier filled his bag with £40,000 cash (as we found out afterwards). The man was quite tubby and wearing a jumper and jeans and left the bank with the minimum of fuss with no-one but Josie and the cashier knowing what had occurred.

Josie was not a 'panicker' and followed the robber out of the bank and across the street before he continued towards St Peter's Square and Oxford Street. As she passed our branch she dived through the door and shouted that someone had just robbed Lloyds Bank at gunpoint and was going towards Oxford Street and she was following so call the police. Before anyone could tell her not to be stupid she was off down the street after him.

Our robber now stopped for a moment and pulled a leather jacket from down his jumper and put it on and zipped it up becoming not a tubby man in a jumper but a thin man in a leather jacket !!

The man continued his escape without noticing Josie following and turned on Oxford Street before coming to his getaway vehicle. A pushbike! Probably not a bad idea in a city centre. The bike was chained to a piece of street furniture with a combination lock. Obviously he didn't want it to be pinched as he visited the bank to rob it and felt that you just couldn't trust people.

As he fumbled with his lock a police van came haring up the street. Josie thought it was coming to her and so she jumped out into the road and was nearly flattened by the police van skidding to a halt. They were on their way to another incident. A burly policeman jumped out of the van and shouted to Josie, "What the hell do you think you are doing?" to which she replied whilst pointing at the man up the street bent over his bike, "It's him !"

The policeman shouted "It's him, what?" and spread his arms. "He's just robbed Lloyds Bank and he's got a gun" shouts Josie. The man now realises that several policemen are running towards him and whilst wrestling him to the ground, shots are fired. OK it was later revealed that it was a starting pistol but if you don't know this at the time......

The man is arrested and the Manchester Evening News covered the story. Proving that fact is always stranger than fiction the robber turned out to be a security guard at the Arndale Centre (Intu now). And there's more, he was getting married the following week! You really couldn't make this stuff up.

Jokes abounded for weeks in the branch about Wedding Dress for sale, never worn or engagement ring for sale etc. There is never any sympathy for someone who has tried to rob you no matter what their circumstances. I have known people to never be able to work on the counter again or having to retire ill having been involved in robbery situations. Josie in the meantime received a £4000 reward from Lloyds Bank as their policy was to pay out 10% of any money recovered in a robbery so all's well that ends well!

IAN MASON

Working with Ken, there were many laughs, but mostly just small incidents. When I left Chester for Glasgow, Barry Walsh, then manager, approached me on my last day around 4.45 with a concerned face and asked if I could carry out a Commercial Mortgage interview, to which I said, "you must be joking". He told me I was the only one qualified. Commercial mortgages were as rare as hens' teeth and I was in a bit of a flap going to collect the customer. Barry told me just to interview her in the small alcove opposite the counter. With trepidation, I sat down with the customer, a young lady, and starts completing an Enquiry Form. When we got to the nature of the business she stood up, started taking off her clothes, and said "exotic dancer".

As my jaw dropped, I looked across to see see about twenty giggling faces at the counter. The oldest trick in the book......the stripogram!!

DAVID JARRATT

This is briefly mentioned but is told much better by David;

In the run up to the merger with the Halifax, many meetings took place between the soon to be vanquished and the victors, (the reader can decide who was which) . These were often distinguished by posturing and attempts at one upmanship by the protagonists, on a grand scale.

I should explain that it was a ritual at the Leeds executive committee meetings that coffee would be served at the table by one of the executives, playing the part of a humble waiter. At one important planning meeting at Halifax, one of the Leeds executives decided it would impress his new peers to carry on this tradition. The coffee was laid out in glass jugs on hot plates on a trolley at the side of the plush and deeply yellow carpeted conference room. Before anyone could move, my Leeds colleague announced that he would serve the coffee to everyone himself and leapt to his feet to pull the coffee laden trolley closer to the conference table.

"No, don't" people cried out, "yes I insist, it's what we do at the Leeds". "Stop, stop " the cries continued unabated. As the trolley moved inexorably away from the wall, so the flexes attaching the hot plates to the plug in the wall pulled tighter and tighter till with a gurgling crash, the hot plates and their passengers were jerked high into the air and came crashing down to the floor in a steamy brown torrent. A corporate groan filled the air as thousands of pounds worth of best Wilton and light oak panelling were drenched with hot black coffee. As a crash to precede the subsequent demise and crash of the Halifax itself, this incident was strangely prophetic though fortunately nowhere near as avoidable.

Many thanks to all of those who contributed. I have to confess that I lost a couple of stories along the way. Many apologies if yours wasn't in the book or this section.

A special mention for John Moseley who came me lots of stories some of which didn't make the final text. Also Peter Jeffs whose story I used but did not credit to protect the innocent.

Paul Duffin

APPENDIX 2
WHERE ARE THEY NOW?
(WRITTEN BY THEMSELVES WITH ONLY VERY LIGHT EDITING)

Mark Waterhouse

After the merger with the Halifax I was posted to Huddersfield as District Manager before moving to the Isle of Man as Managing Director of Halifax International (Isle of Man) Limited. This was the old Leeds Permanent operation and it was great to see the Leeds culture still flourishing on the Island. After a couple of years I took over the Jersey operation of Halifax International and merged the two offshore operations into one legal entity. When the Bank of Scotland merger happened I took the opportunity to leave HBOS and stay on the Island where eventually I became CEO of Zurich Bank International Limited. During my time on the Island I was President of the Bankers Association for many years. This is the trade body which represents all banks here on the Island. I am still President of the local centre of the London Institute of Banking and Finance which is the old Chartered Institute of Banking, looking after the educational needs of bankers and other finance professions. I'm now semi-retired with a number of Non-Executive Director positions and also a Board Member of the local financial services regulator, The Isle of Man Financial Services Authority which keeps me very busy. I am also on the local committee of the Institute of Directors and contactable on LinkedIn.

John Moseley

I retired aged 58 at the end of 2016 after 39 years in the saddle. Such was Lloyds skill with maths they didn't figure that they were giving me two years money to not do two years' work. A mistake the old Leeds would never have made.

I continue to live on the Wirral where I moved in 1987. Having spent the last years of my career running up and down the country for Lloyds Wealth Management training team. I now spend my time running up and down the country in my caravan or on my bike. Oh and I do still do a little work (some would say "he only ever did a little work") delivering cars. Clearly running up and down the country is my thing.

A regular attendee at Rhosneigr John can be contacted on 07785 111316 or peterjmoseley@gmail.com

Julie Walker-Pygott

I joined Leeds Perm straight from school in 1975 aged 16 and after 34 years service took voluntary redundancy on 4th April 2009.

My first job almost ended before it began as due to swapping handbags at the last minute I turned up to my new job with my bank details or national insurance number! Joan McCarthy Personnel Manager told me unless I got these today I would NOT be starting my new job! I had to contact my Mum at work; she caught 2 buses into Leeds and managed to get the documentation needed just in the nick of time!

My first job was that of junior clerk in the writing up section of the Investment Dept. We had 1 VDU and 1 telephone to share between 25 staff who were all aged 16-18 and straight out of school! Lifetime memories were made here and several of us are still in touch some 43 years later! We enjoyed joining the marketing team on The Leeds Perm bus for the annual Lord Mayors Parade handing out Savings sticks, balloons and carrier bags sporting our say the Leeds and your smiling t shirts!

I was also lucky enough to go to Fanhams Hall in Ware. Here I met branch staff from all over the country, we had guest speakers and various workshops, my favourite being when we were asked to produce a tv advert for a rival Building Society, I remember it so well! We made up a song based on the Eurovision song Boom Bang a bang-here was our version to be sung to the tune of Boom Bang a bang:-

Come closer come closer and listen
The Midlands got something you're missing
Our rivals are constantly hissing
At what we can offer to you
It's called the Boom Bond account, Boom Bond account-
income for you
Boom bond account, Boom Bond account high interest too"

Needless to say I never did end up in marketing!

Weekend school in Scarborough was also a good annual
event along with the AGM where if you were lucky you got
asked to be a steward and got to stay overnight at the Queens
hotel!

I worked in most areas of Investment Dept before joining the
newly found Visa Dept. I then took a year out on mat leave
before returning to the newly named Savings Services where I
worked until merger.

My last role was that of senior operations Manager in Secured
Lending before taking voluntary redundancy in 2009.

I then worked for West Yorkshire Police in the HR dept for 5
years before retiring in 2014 to be a full time Nana to my 2
gorgeous grandchildren!

Alan Todd

My Leeds career started at Barrow in Furness followed by
Preston and NW Regional Office. First managerial post was
Prescot, where I not only met Paul for the first time, but also
ended up with Steve Shakeshaft billeted in the room above
the branch. I moved on to Nelson, but three years later I
moved back to Paul's Warrington Regional office as one of
Shakey's AIS team. This involved covering branches in
Lancashire and Cumbria, where apparently I caused fear and
consternation amongst financial advisers and mortgage
advisers when I turned up to observe their interviews. I still

hold that this was the best job I ever had. Later came the Halifax, and then Lloyds, until by 2014 I'd had enough by and escaped via early retirement. For the last year and a half I've enjoyed worked as a porter at Warren and Wignall, auctioneers and valuers in Leyland.

Peter Maskrey

Now happily married & retired and living in Audley, near Newcastle-under-Lyme & Chairman of the local Cricket Club in Bignall End where my Son plays. Also still one of the regular Rhosneigr boys and breakfast chef.

David George

After deciding to leave the Leeds, Dave set up camp in the N&P and then Abbey National. Since 2000, academic life and doctoral research has resulted in lecturing positions at UCLa

Ian Mason

After Chester I worked in Glasgow and Ayrshire as a BM then moved to Financial Services as an adviser and manager. I retired aged 56 and worked in various jobs after that ranging from a Telephone Mortgage Adviser to Pharmacy delivery person! At 61, I think I am now fully retired and have three children and three granddaughters with another grandchild on the way.

Lorna Davies (Baddeley)

Say 'the Leeds and your smiling' was such an apt message for my time spent working at the Leeds Permanent Building Society. I think back to those times and immediately smile as I reminisce on such happy and fond memories. The stresses and strains of work were made less so by the fun and laughter that went hand in hand.

The Regional Office in Warrington was certainly transformed into a happier place when Paul Duffin arrived with his brummy accent and long standing 'mates' in tow, Andy Bates and Ken Brown spring immediately to mind. Peter Maskrey soon joined that inner circle!

Working in those dingy offices above the Warrington branch were soon a thing of the past when we moved into the swanky new office at St James Court. Coming together as an Area team had its trials and tribulations, but once personal egos were forgotten we were soon a formidable team and named ourselves the 'A' team - always finishing off our party nights with Tina Turner's 'Simply the Best' and we were!

The pride of the team when we were out and about in our uniforms, particularly over a lunch time if the girls all went out together - was the equivalent of seeing the Virgin Air Hostesses now walk through an airport - we were impressive and proud to be representing such a warm, friendly and customer driven organisation.

Cheryl Winter (Turley)

The best advice I received in financial services was from my wonderful manager, Phil Moss North West Training Manger. My boyfriend of only 6 months had proposed and I said I needed to think!!!! Well it was a holiday romance and I lived in Chester - he lived in London. Seemed a bit of a risk to me. I thought about it all week, feeling ill and worrying. Finally Phil called me into his room and asked what's wrong. My story came out. Phil asked me what my answer was 'yes' I said. So he said go get on a train and tell him. So I did, there and then, at about 11.00am on a Monday morning. I drove to Warrington Station hopped on a train to London, then a bus then a taxi and finally said 'yes'. We have been married 23 years and have 2 amazing daughters. Best ever financial advice.

 Now I am a Yorkshire girl living round the corner from Paul in Wetherby. I run my own business as a coach for those with dyslexia, ADHD and autism in the workplace. And still in touch with loads of the Leeds Ladies from the North West Regional Office.

Charles Wycks

I retired when HBOS was absorbed into Lloyd's and now live with Helen in Boltby, North Yorkshire where I play a lot of average golf and try to paint landscapes in oils and watercolours.

Contact charleswycks@btinternet.com

Gail Taylor (Roberts)

Well I have super fond memories of my days at The Leeds and still remember joining you and Lorna in that little office upstairs as a young 18 year old and here I am nearly 30 years later □ Still now keep in touch with the girls and met up with Debbie a couple months back for lunch.

I am now the very proud parent of 3 children, Chloe 22, Holly, 17 and Clark 15, I took a career break of a few years from the then Halifax to look after the little ones and became a Childminder then when I went back to work at the Halifax decided it wasn't for me anymore so I needed a change.

So I juggled home life with shift work and spent 10 years working for the Police in the Control Room/999 operator and for the last 2 years to the present day working on the front desk of a busy Police Station....no 2 days are the same !

Oh and soon to celebrate a Silver Wedding Anniversary with Will .....how did I get to this age? lol

Gail Andrews

I joined the Leeds Permanent Building Society on the old YTS (youth training scheme) back when I was 17 years old. It wasn't long before the Leeds Permanent, took me off the YTS and offered me my first permanent job, I was grateful, delighted and excited when I received my offer of employment, and I will never forget reading in my offer letter, that my annual salary was going to be the grand sum of £5,500 per annum. In those days that was a lot of money, especially to me at 17.

I worked as the office junior, but soon found my feet in the personnel department reporting to the personnel officer, Angela. Once I had grasped the filing for over 500+ employee's I was promoted to Personal Assistant to the Personnel Manager. This was something I was very proud of and felt like I'd earned my stripes in the office with the other ladies. I absolutely loved my time working within that office. I formed friendships with people who I still keep in touch with today, and now being 45, I am older than the then 'older ladies in the office'. It was the best grounding I had and was so upset when we merged with the Halifax and we were all deployed elsewhere. I secured a job in the call centre in Warrington, but it just didn't feel the same, the family feel had gone. At the Leeds we had the best social events, and it did feel like one big happy family.

I soon left the Halifax, firstly working for Virgin Atlantic as cabin crew, then the NHS in their recruitment department, then a photographer for a modelling agency. I eventually found my niche working in education recruitment. I have been doing this for the past 13 years; I have gone from consultant to Branch Manager, Regional Manager and I am now the Director of my own company. The office environment I have created and my ethos is to work in a happy place, my office reminds me of my time with the Leeds Permanent Building Society.

Grace Broadhurst (Ruleman)

I joined the Leeds in January 1988 and joined the area team just as you moved to Wilderspool Causeway in September 1989, although I still clearly , very clearly remember the interview with Paul, David and Phil at the old office above the branch for the new role of North West Area Sales Training Manager.

They were truly great times and I couldn't believe it when I was given the job as I was the newest and youngest MT! With

Andy Bullough , John McCarfrae, a couple of years on the scheme ahead ... any way I will always be grateful for that opportunity and space to grow.

Although the Leeds was only 6 years for me before merger with the Halifax and now of course Lloyds they have always been remembered with great fondness for the people, ethics and spirit, truly the best times.

The breakfasts at Wilderspool , Steve Shakeshaft's diet, when you played the Carpenters when he came into the office, trips to Northern Ireland with David and John Edleston, it only seems like yesterday, and the famous Christmas parties at Fiddlers Ferry.
From Area office I moved to Rochdale branch as Manager after Ian Henderson until the merger with Halifax and they too were great times with a great team, some of whom are still with Lloyds.

Where I am now ... well still with the bank and appointed as Head of Business Process in September 2017 where I report to our very own Gordon Edwards!! Who is still Flash Gordon to me! He is now Business Design Director.

I have four amazing children, three boys and one girl aged 19-12.

I remember that you always had an open door, I knew I could contact you at any time t you also trusted me to get on and do my job by being the best I could be. You also said don't take or leave a job because of the manager and that has helped me make some right choices I probably wouldn't have made otherwise.

Derek Newton

I live in Harrogate and having moved around after leaving The Leeds in 1995, I worked for an IFA outfit for over 3 years before joining what is now the College of Policing, then part of the Home Office. I took retirement from there and my wife and

I worked as holiday reps abroad for 5 seasons, amongst other things. Hard work but fascinating - customer service but not as we knew it, Jim! I've also had some acting and voiceover work during those years since leaving The Leeds, whenever the opportunity arose and I got the job that is, which wasn't often enough.!

Sarah Wood (Milner)

Having spent many years working (using the term working loosely!) as a PA for various executive members of The Leeds including Paul Duffin, Charles Wycks, Bob Humphrey's, and Paul Martin to name but a few, I moved to the Halifax Independent Financial Advisors regional office in Wetherby. On realising that Head Office could actually run efficiently without me I decided to opt for voluntary redundancy when it was offered! I now divide my time between my husband, our 2 children and my Labradors in a leafy suburb of Leeds!

Stewart Taylor

I stayed with the Halifax mainly working from Copley which was a dreadful commute) until July 31st 1999 when I took advantage of the voluntary redundancy package. I then had a week's holiday before starting work with Bupa officially based in Staines but working mostly from Leeds heading up the IT activity for the care homes business. After a number of relatively minor changes in role I moved into Procurement in 2006 where I stayed as Head of Procurement (primarily for the care homes until the end of March 2015 before taking semi retirement and continuing 3 days per week acting as Procurement Lead on most of Bupa's acquisitions and disposals. This allowed me the spare time I needed to be the Captain of the Harrogate & District Society of Golf Captains in 2015/16. I retired fully at the end of January 2018 and am now getting used to being fully retired after 8 months which has included a lot of travelling (e.g 5 weeks in New Zealand to start with) and a fair amount of golf. I am also currently the President of Knaresborough GC for 2018 & 2019 and I am also now the Secretary of the Harrogate & District Society of

Golf Captains. These responsibilities and helping my wife to look after our grandson 1 day a week keep me fairly busy

Andy Bates

No matter how hard I tried to escape, I always ended up working and living near to Paul and Sue! In the end I gave up and for the last 26 years, I have been living in Knaresborough, a few miles down the road from the Duffins. My wife Terri left Lloyds 12 years ago and has worked for the famous Betty's ever since. Our daughter, Alison married this year, so it has been a very busy time just lately.

I finally left the Halifax at the end of 2008 and 'retired' for two years. When I decided to go back into the world of work, I made a career decision not to go back into financial services in order to try something different. Immediately I was offered a job......back in Financial Services with an IFA network. I moved to another small network in 2014 and I still work there part time. If ever I get around to it, there is a book based on my experiences. The trouble is, no-one would believe it!

We have had the good fortune to have been friends with Paul and Sue for over 40 years. Paul and I still have a night at the pub every week and I have seen at very close hand the remarkable way he has dealt with the deterioration of his sight and hearing. He remains as positive and cheerful as ever and when he finds he cannot do something anymore, he finds something else to do, hence his becoming an author.

As I always say to him "whenever I am unwell, I always remember that there is someone worse off than myself......and it's always you!"